Shadow of TERROR

Shadow of TERROR

Rene Noorbergen

REVIEW AND HERALD® PUBLISHING ASSOCIATION
WASHINGTON, DC 20039-0555
HAGERSTOWN, MD 21740

The author assumes full responsibility for the accuracy of all facts and
quotations as cited in this book.

This book was
Edited by Gerald Wheeler
Designed by Bill Kirstein
Type set: 10.5 Goudy Old Style

PRINTED IN U.S.A.

95 94 93 92 91 90   10 9 8 7 6 5 4 3 2 1

Library of Congress Cataloging-in-Publication Data
Noorbergen, Rene.
    Shadow of terror / Rene Noorbergen.
        p.   cm.
    1. Noorbergen, Rene. 2. World War, 1939-1945—
Underground movements—Netherlands—Groningen. 3. World
War, 1939-1945—Personal narratives, Dutch. 4. World War, 1939-
1945—Children—Netherlands—Groningen. 5. Foreign correspon-
dents—United States—Biography. 6. Groningen (Netherlands)
—History. I. Title.
D802.N42G766   1990
940.53'49212—dc20
                                                      90-42567
                                                          CIP

ISBN 0-8280-0576-1

Other books by Rene Noorbergen

Jeane Dixon: My Life and Prophecies
You Are Psychic
Ellen G. White—Prophet of Destiny
Charisma of the Spirit
The Ark File
Programmed to Life
The Soul Hustlers
Secrets of the Lost Races
The Deathcry of an Eagle
Living With Loss
Nostradamus—Invitation to a Holocaust
Nostradamus Predicts World War III
Treasures of the Lost Races
The Ten Million Dollar Hostage
A.D. 2000—A Book About the End of Time
Noah's Ark Found—The End of the Search

A WORD OF THANKS AND APPRECIATION

Memory alone is insufficient when it comes to recalling all the events that produced this manuscript. The valuable help extended by the following individuals and organizations is greatly appreciated.

1. Netherlands Institute for War Documentation
2. Mr. J.F.J. Vogt of the archives of the city of Groningen
3. Mr. Jan Pijlman of the Department of Internal Affairs of the county of Texel
4. Mr. Piet Boonstra, press photographer in the city of Groningen during World War II
5. The Netherlands Broadcasting Corporation
6. The Netherlands Television Corporation
7. Mr. Gijs Davids

There is no way in which the contributions made by these people or organizations can be ranked. Their photographs, personal recollections, and documentation helped make this book a factual document.

DEDICATION

Lovingly dedicated to
my personal hero of the war years,
MY DAD,
whose compassion kept many alive,
and H.R.H. PRINCE BERNHARD,
whose leadership of the resistance movement
kept our courage aflame.

RENE

CONTENTS

INTRODUCTION

World War II scorched the globe with a murderous fire half a century ago, and its shocking events still remain deeply engraved in the minds of those who managed to live through it. It only takes a word, a song, a whiff of a familiar odor, or a photograph to recall its memories from that unfathomable mental abyss where we store all our old and painful experiences. And when some of them surface to our consciousness, no matter how long they have lain there quietly, they still have the ability to cause pain and sorrow.

Each of us from that generation have our own particular memories of the years 1940-1945. To me, however, they are closely entwined with the horror and fear that replaced an important part of my childhood, for when the invaders came rolling across the border, they robbed me of five innocent years when fear should have been just a word in a book and not an actual experience. But those turbulent years at the same time developed a closeness in our family that made the dark days bearable.

The events recorded on the following pages actually happened. They show that reality is often wilder and more frightening than anything even the most vivid human imagination can conjure up. Believe me, recalling many of the tragic incidents portrayed in this book still has the ability to transform peaceful nights into terrifying nightmares . . . even now, 50 long years later.

Rene Noorbergen
Collegedale, Tennessee

CHAPTER ONE

A Mysterious Affinity

Standing nervously at the edge of a narrow strip of farmland between a dusty country road and what appeared to have been a former prison camp of the Third Reich, I had felt like an unwelcome intruder on history. Leaning in deep thought against the left front fender of my light blue MG convertible, I now held a handful of dirt, trying to identify the faint chemical odor I kept smelling. I was sure it wasn't fertilizer. It was more like chlorine or lime, but what bothered me even more than the mysterious scent was the barren patch of soil at my feet. Why did I feel so edgy?

Glancing down at the ground, I wondered what lay hidden beneath the soil that smelled so much like disinfectant. Bodies maybe? If so, I could well imagine what the decayed flesh might look and smell like after so many years. Could I possibly be standing on an unknown mass grave dating back to when the defeated German war machine had hurriedly obliterated all traces of those who witnessed its cruelty? What really was the story behind this camp where I had received such an unwelcome reception only minutes before? What sinister secrets did it protect? Why did I feel so strangely drawn to the place? I was determined to find out.

It had all begun as a magazine assignment. I had returned to my native Holland a week or so before to enjoy a well-earned vacation from studying history and journalism at La Sierra College in southern California. Within a short time after arriving at my parental home in the ancient city of Groningen I received an unexpected phone call from Henk Benda, an old friend and editor in chief of the Dutch illustrated magazine *Vizier*. He wondered whether I'd be interested in checking out a rumor about a youth camp in the northwestern section of West Germany—not far across the border from my hometown. Now, as I stared down at the barren area near my feet, my mind kept drifting to our conversation and the details of the assignment he had given me. "They told me that the camp's windows are covered by rusty iron bars. Check it out, will you?" he had said after giving me the necessary facts. By now, I too had become suspicious—a youth camp with iron bars on its windows?

A week after Benda contacted me, I had driven toward one of the northernmost border crossings between Holland and Germany, my destination a camp for the rehabilitation of East German youth who had escaped from their Communist masters soon after the division of Germany. The influx of the young refugees had prompted the West German government to initiate a program to recondition them before turning them loose on West German society. The authorities decided that youth rehabilitation camps were the answer.

For me, it was not a pleasant assignment. World War II had only been over a little more than 10 years, and my distrust of anything German and my continuing repugnance with the so-called "super race" had always kept me from accepting projects involving Germany. But a youth camp with iron bars across the windows made me too suspicious to turn it down. My innate distrust only fanned on my interest, and I was anxious to discover whatever secrets the camp was covering up.

Even after 10 years my memories of the war years were still vivid and I could not repress them. Each time I crossed the border into Germany, frightening images of marching soldiers flooded my mind. I could still hear the heavy guttural sounds of hundreds of Nazi voices singing German war songs as they passed my house.

As I slammed on the brakes at the German customs shack, I felt that same fear and abhorrence surfacing again. Seeing the customs officials in their familiar old Wehrmacht-style uniforms and hearing them bark their sharp commands from the hut had released a flow of disturbing memories that I thought I had buried deep within my subconscious.

"Anything to declare?" the guard growled at me. His face was a composite of all the other angular German faces I had known—all merged into one. How I hated these men for making me relive the past all over again. Would I ever be free from the memories? Would I and the others my age always continue to despise Germans so intensely. Who were these moss-green uniformed men that the mere sight of one of them could still evoke such hard feelings within me after all those years. Why did they still use the same style uniforms? Were they perhaps leftovers from the war?

The rush of air on my face as I drove off, ignoring their demanding questions, was filled with the fragrance of freshly harvested fields and the promise of new life in a land that had bred death so long for so many.

The toll Germany had extracted from my own family would have been much greater than it had been if we had not struggled to stay one danger-laden step ahead of the Gestapo (Gehime Staats Polizei or "Secret State Police"), the feared enforcers of German law who always dressed in long black leather coats and wide brimmed black felt hats. They had absolute power over life and death.

My Uncle Gijs had been one tragedy. His capture followed a few hours after the Gestapo's failure to grab my father, his older brother. Shortly before the end of the war we were having a quiet dinner when a heavy rap on the front door announced the arrival of unexpected visitors. While dad unlatched one of the windows overlooking the courtyard and jumped out, I quickly ran down the hallway, opened the door, and stared into the most dreaded face in all of Groningen. It was Lehnhoff, the feared torturer of the local Gestapo. Looking past his shoulder, I could see his driver leaning against the open door of his black Mercedes, holding a pistol in his right hand while his left thumb was hooked into his gun belt. The two Dutch Nazi stormtroopers in their dull black uniforms who waited casually a few steps behind Lehnhoff stepped aside when he began to question me.

"I want to see your father," he demanded.

"He's not home," I answered loudly, trusting that he had already crossed the courtyard and had successfully crawled into the granary next door and hoping that my mother would be able to hear the conversation and signal him to keep moving.

Lehnhoff grinned menacingly. "You know who I am. You have seen me before! When you see your father, tell him to report to me in the morning," he continued in his gruff voice while turning on his heels and walking down the three steps to the sidewalk and back to his Mercedes. Not wanting to return to headquarters without his intended prey, he decided to try his luck at my uncle's house a few kilometers away. After his troopers had checked out the premises without results, he decided to wait it out. Leaning against his car, he kept a sharp eye on the street corner of the E. Thomassen A. Theusinglaan.

An hour later a solitary bicycler turned the corner into the A. P. Fokkerstraat. Signaling to his men to back him up, Lehnhoff grabbed Gijs' arm just as my uncle slowed down in front of his house and swung his leg backward over the rear wheel to jump off his bike.

Lehnhoff had a victim, for inside the box securely tied to the luggage carrier, he found a short-wave transmitter—contraband punishable by death in a concentration camp. We never knew exactly why the Gestapo threw out its net to catch the two Noorbergen brothers, but it was obvious they suspected that they were members of the underground. They just needed proof, and now they had it.

Within minutes they had thrown Gijs into the car and hauled him away to Gestapo headquarters for interrogation. We never saw him again. The news of his capture reached us later that evening, and we trembled, knowing what he could be enduring at that very moment. As a radioman for the underground, he would be tortured to provide the names of his contacts before being executed or placed on a transport to a concentration camp. Fear gripped our hearts, for dad and I remembered hearing muffled screams drifting out of the open second floor window of Gestapo headquarters at the Grote Markt as we had walked by the building a few days earlier. The cries of the tortured could still be heard even over the loud playing of the classical music that the Germans customarily used to drown out the screams of their victims. Although we were all aware of the suffering that went on in that building, we were totally helpless to do anything about it. We had heard that one of their prisoners, his fingers mangled, had broken free and jumped through a second story window to escape his tormentors. But all that concerned us now was my Uncle Gijs. What could they be doing to him?

From the stories we had heard, we knew there was no limit to the suffering the Germans inflicted on their prisoners, and it wasn't until

Gijs Noorbergen, the author's uncle, who died after being captured by the Gestapo.

after the war that we received the first news about my uncle's fate. A survivor of one of the concentration camps told us of seeing Gijs with only one leg. The other had been sawed off either in Groningen or after his arrival at a small concentration camp not far from the Dutch-German border. The ex-prisoner had not been able to tell us the name of the camp. Now standing at the site of the former rehabilitation camp in Germany, I began to wonder. Could there be a connection between the barracks, the window bars, Gijs, and this vegetationless area at my feet?

Suddenly the bright afternoon sky darkened and a gusty wind swirled in through the camp, bringing with it large drops of rain that splattered against my face. But as quickly as it had started, the wind calmed and the storm was over. Overhead the thick blanket of clouds that had moved in to obscure the last few slivers of sunlight now separated to release the warm rays of the sun once more. Was this a foreshadow of the news that awaited me here—sad and distressful, then relief?

Leni, my beautiful companion who had accompanied me on the

assignment, and I had left the men outside the German customs shack choking in a cloud of dust as we spun off down the road following the black and yellow directional signs. I soon navigated around and through the hundreds of potholes in what formerly had been a farm road. It must have been passable at one time, but the vehicles that once used the road were probably overloaded and too numerous, and today the road was totally in disrepair. To me it suggested that we were beginning to get uncomfortably close to our destination.

I began to wonder why I had accepted the writing assignment in the first place. I knew it hadn't been a favor to Henk Benda. Something else had driven me to take it. But what? It surely hadn't been the money.

Leni's dark blue eyes had been busily scanning the peaceful landscape while I tried to avoid as many holes as possible. Surrounding us were freshly harvested wheat fields that seemed to touch both the Dutch horizon and the billowy cumulus clouds overhead. This was one day when everything would surely go my way. A fascinating assignment, an unexplainable feeling of mounting excitement, and pleasant company—all rolled into one.

It was Leni who had first noticed a number of old wooden barracks far across a newly harvested field on our right. Looking beyond the endless rows of neatly stacked yellow sheaves of wheat drying in the sun, we also noticed an occasional glimmer of reflected sunlight flashing from angular pieces of glass still stuck in broken window frames.

Barely able to avoid a horse-drawn pig manure cart, I was forced to slide into an even narrower side road at the end of what we recognized as the rotted remains of two wooden gateposts. On them someone had fastened a freshly painted sign warning people to keep out.

"*Eintritt verboten,*" it stated in formal German.

Guiding the sleek MG past the posts, carefully skirting the loose strands of rusted barbed wire that reached gracefully on gentle wisps of wind for the car's virgin paint job, we entered the forbidden grounds of the youth rehabilitation camp. Our arrival apparently went unnoticed until I stopped in the middle of a rectangular courtyard lined on either side with bare wooden barracks. We stepped out and looked around, listening for the tell-tale sounds of children. But we heard nothing. No sound of running feet, no happy laughter or singing, nothing disturbed the deathly quiet.

"Didn't you see the sign? *'Eintritt verboten!'* " a man who suddenly appeared in a doorway between two bare window frames now shouted at us. He stood there with his right arm outstretched against the wall and his hand resting casually on a rusty window bar.

Turning to the direction of his voice, I raised my Leica and aimed it at him.

"*Heraus* (Out, away)," he screamed again, then repeated somewhat more politely, "*Gehen Sie heraus,*" while pointing in the direction of the rows of barred and empty windows. Quickly I asked whether it had always been a youth camp, and if so, why the bars and those—I continued pointing, but now at the high wooden observation tower on the far end of the courtyard and also at the four tall posts with the ragged remains of floodlights and iron loudspeaker housings strategically situated at the four corners of the courtyard. It did not take much imagination for me to visualize black-uniformed SS guards on the watchtower and observation platform crouched behind mounted Mauser machine guns and to hear the familiar war-time command, "*Achtung . . . Achtung!* (Attention!)" and the "*Horst Wessel Lied,*" the Nazi marching song blaring from rusty loudspeakers.

My questions left him speechless, yet his anger was quite evident, for his face had reddened, emphasizing a long pale vertical scar on his cheek that started on the right side of his nose.

"Didn't this used to be a prison camp or a small concentration camp?" I demanded. In reply he vented a flood of curses, during which I learned that I was nothing more than a "*Schweinehund*" (a pig dog) among other things.

Sliding back into the car, I decided to leave before our verbal exchange turned physical. Also I was sure that I had all the answers I needed. Yet I sensed that there was something more to be found. Throwing the car in reverse, I backed out of the courtyard through the barbed-wire gateposts, circled the camp following ruts cut by the farm carts—even making some of my own—and ended up directly behind the barracks. It was there at the edge of a stubble field that I noticed a rough circular area of perhaps 15 meters in diameter. I studied it carefully. The soil was barren all right. Not one blade of grass, nor even a weed grew in it. Kicking some dirt loose with the heel of my shoe, I bent over and scooped up a handful of the dark brown soil and held it close to my face, then rubbed some of it through my fingers. The substance felt like soil, but I still sensed something different about it. Finally I decided it didn't smell right. The sample I examined had a faint chemical odor to it. Not fertilizer—more like chlorine, lime, or a disinfectant.

Suddenly the persistent ringing of a bicycle bell set in motion by the thumb of an impatient farmer jarred me from my concentration. He was telling me in his own way that the front end of my car was obstructing the path. Instantly I seized the unexpected opportunity for another interview.

"Is this a mass grave?" I called out to him while pointing to the ground. "And how about this place?" I continued, gesturing to the barracks. "Was it a prison camp or a concentration camp?"

"Ich weiss nichts davon (I don't know a thing about that)," he stuttered nervously. *"Fragen Sie mich nichts mehr* (Ask me no more). *Ich bin nur ein Bauer* (I am only a farmer)." Then, mumbling a few nasty words under his breath about inquisitive cheeseheads (German vernacular for Dutchmen), he swung his leg over the bike saddle and peddled off, leaving us with our suspicions mounting and a mysterious plot of lifeless soil.

A few days later, with my report in his hands, Henk Benda notified the Dutch government about the find. A suspicious area that close to the border of northern Holland called for an investigation, and, as I suspected, it was a mass grave. An exhumation of the remains revealed that one of the skeletons had only one leg. After further investigation, there was no doubt. We had at long last found Uncle Gijs.

Ten years of wondering, anguish, tears, and frustration were finally over for his wife and son, Bertie, whose chance to really know his father had been brutally taken from him by Hitler's Gestapo.

A few weeks later a courageous resistance fighter finally returned to Groningen in a small lead box—to be buried with full military honors in a special cemetery reserved for slain members of the Dutch underground.

Standing next to my father at the edge of the grave that would receive Gijs' remains, I could see the memories of those terrifying five war years reflected in the tears that rolled down his cheeks. The haunting taps that sounded over his brother's grave gently faded out among the trees of the surrounding forest, and the salvo of gunfire that cracked sharply over the red, white, and blue flag of his country signified the gratitude of his nation. Uncle Gijs was home again.

After the service, Dad and I slowly walked away without looking back. For us the war was finally over, though the anguish and torment resulting from the German occupation would remain with us the rest of our lives. It wasn't just our family who grieved for a loved one that day. There were mourners, whether present or not, for every grave in that "Resistance Fighters Cemetery." Holland had lost thousands at the merciless hands of a tyrannical political philosophy, and that will never be forgotten.

CHAPTER TWO

Unending
Fear

To me, even as an 11-year-old, the German "Blitzkrieg" (lightning war) invasion did not come as a complete surprise. Worries about the possibility of war had already begun the previous summer of 1939. The Eelsings, close friends of ours, and our family had been camping at Norg, a camping resort area about 20 miles from Groningen. One morning the hammer blows of county officials nailing posters to trees and telephone poles jarred us awake. The posters summoned all armed forces reservists to report to their units immediately. The Dutch government had decided on full mobilization because of Germany's expansionist politics and the fear that Hitler would not respect Holland's desire for neutrality.

The date of May 10, 1940, when the war began, will always remain engraved in my mind. Whether awake or asleep, I still remember and react to the memories of that infamous day and the five years that followed.

The identity of the German dictator, Adolf Hitler, had been the subject of much ridicule and speculation in the European press for several years already, as he had been born the illegitimate child of 28-year-old Clara Schiklgruber and her cousin, Alois. Feeling sorry for her and her little boy, a wandering miller named Johan Hiedler decided to marry her. At a later date Adolf adopted the name Hiedler but spelled it Hitler. After moving to Austria, he quit school at the age of 16 because of falling grades, and his dream of becoming an artist ended when he failed the art school entrance exam in Vienna. During

World War I, he enlisted in the German Army and rose to the rank of corporal.

At the end of the First World War, Germany had sunk into a deep economic depression. Young Adolf viewed the Jews and communists as responsible for his country's collapse and joined the budding Nationalist Socialist Workers Party, later known as Nazis. The Party's revolt in the province of Bavaria failed and the government jailed Hitler for treason. While in jail he wrote his famous book, *Mein Kampf,* assisted by his cellmate, Rudolph Hess. In the book he outlined his beliefs and his plans to conquer Europe. He ar-

A childhood photo of Adolf Hitler.

gued that Germans were the highest species of man on earth, and that by avoiding intermarriage with Jews, German children could be images of the Lord and not monstrosities halfway between man and apes. He blamed the Jews as behind all the evils in the world and put the communists in the same category.

Later a Dutch communist, Van der Lubbe, was accused of burning the German parliament building, the Reichtag, on February 27, 1933. I remember that day when as a 5-year-old my little friends and I would jokingly say, *"Van der Lubbe met de kop er af,* (Van der Lubbe without a head)," because we had obviously overheard adults discussing his possible fate.

After the German president, Paul van Hindenburg, appointed Hitler Chancellor of the Republic in 1933, Adolf took dictatorial power and began to rearm Germany in order to take vengeance on the neighboring countries of western Europe for his country's defeat in 1918.

Using the Nazi Nürnberg laws adopted in 1935, he had political opponents of National Socialism and Jews imprisoned in the Dachau concentration camp outside Munich.

Hitler's dream of expansionism—of creating *"lebensraum"* (living space) for his impoverished Germans—began with the reincorporation of the Saar territory and the Rhineland in 1937 followed by the takeover of Austria and Poland in 1939.

* * *

For my family it all began early on the morning of the 10th of May when a shout from my father catapulted me out of bed. "Rene, *word wakker* (wake up). *Het is oorlog!* (It's war). *The Duitsers zijn al onderweg. Ze vechten overal* (The Germans are on the way—they're fighting everywhere)." Within seconds I scrambled down the ladder from my loft bedroom over the kitchen.

It just couldn't be true. The previous evening a school chum and I had spent many hours examining and exchanging our Nazi pictures. For a number of years the German propaganda machine had been busy exporting the Nazi image through music by broadcasting over Radio Berlin appealing two-part harmony military songs, and by enclosing pictures in German export products. Hermann Goering, their Propaganda Minister, was obsessed with capturing the minds of the youth of Europe, and what could be more fascinating to a youngster than to have easy access to brightly colored cards showing men and boys in different flashy uniforms. Even though most European countries had their own Nazi sympathizers, none of their governments were interested in promoting the German militaristic image, so pictures of Hitler and his cabinet including Goering, Goebbels, and Baldur von Schirach in resplendent military attire, as well as the Hitler Jugend (Youth), members of the S.A. (stormtroopers), and SS (the elite army unit) were enclosed within packages of certain German export items. The *maut kaffee* (a coffee substitute made from roasted grain) my mother used to buy at the local health food store contained such pictures. As kids we collected them and exchanged duplicates much the same way children swap baseball cards in the United States.

Now to believe that those nice-looking people on those colorful cards were my enemy was rather confusing to an 11-year-old mind.

Barefooted, I followed my dad down the long marble hallway to the front door of our house. He was already outside when I got there. Fear was in the air as we heard the excited voice of an announcer reading war bulletins that blared out of the radio loudspeaker in our living room. After reaching the vestibule, I pushed open the heavy oak door and saw my father standing at the edge of the sidewalk, talking and gesturing to two of our upholsterers who had come by, wondering whether they should report to work. My father owned a number of furniture stores plus a workshop around the corner where he manufactured and reupholstered furniture.

A pen sketch of the author's childhood home drawn during the early 1920s.

Glancing past them I noticed small groups of grim-faced sailors who had gathered to exchange war news. Spontaneously they began to sing "Wilhelmus," the Dutch national anthem, in an unusual display of emotion and patriotism. It started softly — almost reverently at first — then became louder and more forceful as the tears began to trickle down their weatherbeaten faces. Their voices blended with the morning breeze and mixed with the war bulletins from the radio that my mother had hurriedly placed in the still open doorway.

The news flashes were frightening. The Germans had dropped paratroopers at strategic spots all over the country while the feared Stukas, the German dive-bombers we already knew from newspaper and magazine pictures, were obliterating all Dutch communication centers, military headquarters, and airport runways. The town of Nieuweschans on the Dutch-German border, a mere 30 miles from our home, was also quickly overrun. Yet, everything on the street alongside the canal in front of our house continued at its usual early morning pace. The milkman had just halted his horse-drawn cart to make his delivery next door, and an occasional truck drove by, coming from the direction of the German border. Nothing as yet betrayed the crisis in which Holland found itself, and it would be another thirty minutes before the first signs of the developing national drama became evident and the seriousness of what lay ahead for the nation, penetrated.

View of the author's house and the old gatekeeper's house that burned down in the street fighting that liberated Groningen.

An excited old man came running up to us from the *poortershuisje* (gatekeeper's house) on the left at the edge of the canal. "They're coming," he shouted, gesturing to a Dutch army truck, followed closely by a German motorcycle patrol. Behind them rumbled a personnel carrier filled with heavily armed infantry.

When the Dutch army truck was abreast of our house, it slowed down and the driver leaned toward the open window and shouted, "Get inside quickly, they'll be here any moment!" Ignoring his suggestion, we walked briskly to the rear of the truck and cast a curious glance inside. It was jammed with Dutch soldiers. A bloodstained cloth held against the neck of one of them gave me my first glimpse of the horror of war.

As the truck slowly moved on, the enemy motorcycle patrol behind him screeched to a sudden stop. Singling out a pedestrian whose smiling face showed no fear, the German driver asked how to get to the City Hall. As soon as the patrol heard the directions and veered off out of sight, fists from the bystanders began pummeling the informer's face and head, forcing him to the pavement.

I was only 11, but on that first day of the war I had not only seen my first German soldier but also my very first Dutch traitor.

Later that day we heard that the German State radio had called upon all members of the NSB—the Dutch Nazi party—to support the attackers and assist the invading German army at all cost.

In the week that followed, we learned that the "cooperative" pedestrian was indeed a member of the NSB, and it was our first lesson not to trust anyone until he or she proved otherwise.

Little did I realize then that May 10 would be the beginning of five years of terror, and that within two years it would affect the lives of our entire family. We would be hiding fugitives from the Gestapo and Dutch Nazis, and before the war ended, we'd even be smuggling weapons, Jews, and an SS deserter all over our province. Four and a half years from that very day, my father and I would escape from Gestapo headquarters.

Everyone was at first hopeful that it would be a short-term occupation. Even the German soldiers who passed our home by the thousands that day, crammed into endless convoys of trucks and rattling armored personnel carriers, seemed to think that by crossing into our country, England was just a step away, for one of the two-part harmony songs we heard all day as the columns passed by was *"Und Wir Fahren Gegen Engeland"* (And We Are Traveling Toward England). That song sung so enthusiastically by the thousands of smiling young German soldiers gave us the uneasy feeling that they already considered themselves the victors. Their sense of geography, however, was a little off, for I remember one truck driver hollering at us, "Where does Churchill live? How do we get to his house?" Apparently he didn't know that he would still have to cross the Channel before reaching the shores of England. Those who overheard him laughingly passed it on to the next group on the sidewalk, and before long everyone on the street was chuckling, a welcome relief from the tension and anxiety we all felt. We knew the tears would come soon enough.

What passed that day was only part of the 27 armored divisions of Army Group B that German General von Bock used to attack Holland and Belgium as part of a massive drive against France. At the outset we heard that the German force consisted of a total of 126 divisions, ten of which were panzer (armored) with nearly 3,000 armored vehicles, including 1,000 heavy Tiger tanks. It was days before we found out via the BBC that the total number of divisions deployed for the destruction of Holland, Belgium, Luxembourg, and France was actually 155, and most of their troops had gained their first battle experience during the invasion of Poland the previous September. The ten lightly armed Dutch and the 22 equally unprepared Belgian divisions were no match against such battle-hardened German soldiers.

But even though the Dutch army was outnumbered, it employed several surprise tactics to hinder the German advance. It deliberately breached strategic dikes located in the southwestern part of Holland, flooding the meadows with a few feet of water to disguise the deep irrigation ditches, so as to trap and drown enemy infantry as they swept across the land. It was a desperate move that ruined many crops, but it also destroyed Germans as well.

Further north, other German units had taken control of the locks

German armored troops attacking Holland in May 1940.

at the *Afsluitdijk* (Closing Dike) separating the Zuider Zee from the North Sea. A few Dutch marines who had stayed behind after their main unit had retreated decided on a counter action of their own. Noticing a rubber boat filled with German soldiers near the locks, they slipped undetected down the dike into the water. Swimming under the surface, they slit the boat with their bayonets, and one by one they engaged the soldiers in hand to hand combat in the water, killing them all. Forced ashore at gunpoint by other soldiers, they were taken to the commanding officer of the German unit, who after hearing about the fight and their bravery against overwhelming odds, pulled off his own Iron Cross decoration and pinned it on the uniform of one of the marines.

My little country had been invaded and though it would eventually surrender, its people never stopped scheming and plotting any way they could to destroy their German occupiers.

My impressions of that day are anchored solidly in my mind—the rattling of the passing armor, the singing of the victorious soldiers, and the tramping of the heavy boots of the marching infantrymen. Hearing the frightening sounds and listening to the adults around me discuss what all this would mean to our peaceful way of life was overwhelming.

I recall grabbing my father's hand and asking, "Can we go somewhere—to Assen or Meppel," naming some small towns close by.

"No! No! That won't do," he answered nervously, shaken by his inability to safeguard his small family from the horrors that obviously lay ahead. Having been responsible for earning a living for his family—consisting of his mother and five younger brothers and sisters since he was 16 until he married at age 21, it was his nature to take charge, but this situation was different. No matter how desperately he wanted to reassure us that everything would be all right, he was facing too many unknowns and he was scared.

I remember writing in my diary that night, "I don't know what will happen now. Dad is so old already and mom too. I hope they will survive this. He is already 40 years old, and she is 42." Thinking back to that day, I clearly remember her—about five feet tall with raven black hair, braided and fastened on the top of her head, with tears filling her large blue eyes. Her nervousness was obvious and evidenced by red blotches high on her cheeks.

Being the youngest in her family and nicknamed *Pukkie* (meaning "little one" in the dialect of the province of Groningen), she was her father's favorite child, and she adored him. He had been born in Germany, and even though the Germans were now our enemies, she was unable to hate them that first day. After all, "they" were her father's people! My dad's reaction, however, was far from sentimental. He saw them as a dangerous threat to his peaceful existence. At 40, he was in his prime, with thinning blond hair that seemed to be typical for a man that age. I thought he was already an old man. The fourth member of our family was my 16-year-old sister, Dina, who, with her blonde wavy hair and blue eyes, caught the immediate attention of the soldiers as they passed our house. Just one more thing for my father to worry about.

It was clear to me that Dad knew only a little more than I did about what was happening. I can still picture him in my mind, leaning over with his ear to the radio, listening intently each night for several weeks to the reports about the German slaughter in Poland and the oppressive rule that followed the initial battles.

"Will it be like Poland, Dad?" I now asked him. He didn't reply.

As I crawled into bed that first night and heard the continuous grinding and rattling sounds on the street caused by the tanks and personnel carriers, it was enough for me to realize we would be under the heel of the Germans for a long time, for there were just too many of them. The singing and the sound of marching and heavy machinery rattling continued throughout the night and was still there when I went down for breakfast. By now it was evident that there was no way out. Little did we know that our government on which we based our only hope for survival had already made preparations for the escape of its cabinet members and the royal family on a British destroyer.

The radio news service continued to broadcast battle reports of the fighting that still raged throughout the country for the next four days. Finally, as punishment for not surrendering, the German Luftwaffe (air force) rained bombs on the city of Rotterdam on May 14, destroying the entire city center and killing thousands of innocent people. That one raid left about 80,000 of the survivors homeless, and the German High Command threatened to do the same to other major cities, such as Amsterdam, Utrecht, and The Hague, unless all armed resistance ceased. Their pressure tactics worked. The ruins of Rotterdam were still smoldering when the High Command of the Dutch Army surrendered at 11:00 a.m. on May 15, 1940.

Even the British Expeditionary Force in France was unable to stop the onslaught. It was a no-win situation, and they faced total annihilation. The British government immediately decided on a withdrawal of their forces and ordered them to retreat to the beach of Dunkirk, a seaport on the northern coast of France. While under constant air attack from the Germans, an armada of vessels ranging from destroyers to rowboats began evacuating the British and French troops on May 27.

The day after our war started, May 11, Uncle Gijs, Dad's younger brother, along with a friend of his, stopped by to ask my father to join a budding resistance movement, the "underground," known in Dutch as the *ondergrondse*. Even though pockets of resistance fighters sprang up all over the country, the movement did not officially organize until the beginning of 1941 when it published the first underground newspapers. They started as single mimeographed sheets bearing the names of *"Vrij Nederland"* (Free Netherlands), *"Parool"* (Password) and *"Trouw"* (Loyalty). (These resistance bulletins eventually evolved after the war into major national newspapers and still carry the same names.) The resistance organizations hindered and sabotaged the activities of the German occupation forces as well as the puppet Dutch civilian administration run by members of the Dutch Nazi Party.

Quite soon most Dutch citizens either became involved in the resistance or supported the movement as active sympathizers, and our family was no different. Being firmly anti-Nazi and fiercely loyal to our country, all of us naturally desired to participate in any activity that would obstruct the occupation. Even though she was in her middle 70s, my paternal grandmother also did her part. By selling and delivering packets of coffee and tea to individuals all over our section of the city, she disguised her role as courier for the underground and successfully delivered verbal messages and instructions whenever needed. Who would suspect an old woman carrying a shopping bag filled with coffee and tea. Nobody apparently, for neither the Germans nor the Dutch Nazis ever stopped and searched her. Even her husband (my grandfather), from whom she was separated and who lived in Zaandam, a city close to Amsterdam, also worked in the resistance. This we only discovered after the war when my dad recognized his father's photo on a counterfeit I.D. card bearing another name at a touring resistance exhibit.

We had been invaded, and everyone, no matter how old or young, fought back in his own way.

I was too young to be in on that initial meeting at our house, but caught enough of the conversation to understand the meaning of the discussion. By listening through a crack in the door, I heard Uncle Gijs say, "We have a case of rifles and a few boxes of shells we would like to hide for a while until we need to distribute them."

"I can hide all you've got," my father replied.

Later that day my uncle arrived at our three-story-high combination furniture warehouse and repair shop with two long wooden crates on the loading platform of a *bakfiets* (a cargo-carrying tricycle). "I sure hope they don't slip loose on the way up," I remember thinking as I watched them being tied onto the steel hook of the swaying

The author's paternal grandmother, who was a courier in the Dutch underground.

cable. With my legs straddling the crates, I was hoisted up with them, after which we pulled them onto the third floor loading platform. Before stepping off the crates, I cast a hurried glance to the street below where Uncle Gijs had become involved in a conversation with a soldier who was maneuvering his truck into the German motorpool garage next door. "That *Mof* (Dutch slang for German) had better not look up and recognize the size and shape of those boxes. We'll be arrested for sure," I muttered to myself. I seemed to be worried all the time.

The city of Groningen was on the bombing run from England to the German ports of Bremerhaven, Emden, and Hamburg, and not long after the beginning of the occupation, the Germans erected a number of searchlights and heavy anti-aircraft guns near the new

Grote Markt, Groningen's central marketplace, with its thirteenth-century Martini tower. The Gestapo headquarters is on the right. The picture was taken before street fighting destroyed the city's center.

canal locks a mile from our house. Those guns, combined with the Messerschmidt and Heinkel fighter planes stationed at nearby Eelde Airport, soon made Groningen a hotspot for the British and American bombers. Often, when attacked over the city, the Allied pilots opened their bomb bays and released their explosive loads over the unsuspecting city. None of us minded the occasional bombs falling because we knew the pilots couldn't help it. They were our friends, and we didn't hold it against them when they found themselves forced to lighten their loads to escape the cross beams of the German searchlights and the cannon fire of the fighter planes. However, after a few raids like this, our fully packed suitcases sat permanently in the hallway just in case we needed to escape quickly. Fortunately for us, the incendiary bombs always struck somewhere else in the city, blocks away from us. It was about this time that the authorities set up air-raid shelters throughout the city.

The Allied air raids, however, did not evoke as much fear as the mere mention of the "Scholtenshuis," a large gray stone structure that had once been the home of Groningen's wealthiest industrial family. Situated on the Grote Markt, the city's central square, its new occupants were the Gestapo, and every Groninger knew that whoever entered that building would probably never be seen again. They just disappeared. Across a narrow street, standing straight and 309 feet high, was the thirteenth-century St. Martin's church tower that my father had climbed every night during the last few months preceding the war to watch for approaching German planes. Diagonally from the tower was an imposing sixteenth-century building, its dignified facade now draped with swastika banners two stories high. Here the German High Command for Groningen had taken over.

During that early phase of the war, the Dutch tolerated the German soldiers but did not fear them like we did the Gestapo and the Dutch Nazi stormtroopers charged with maintaining state security. To them almost anything could be interpreted as being a threat to the so-called "Aryan" race. The basic philosophy of the Germans was that they were superior to any other people, and the Dutch stormtroopers used the concept to settle many personal grudges. People were simply dragged off into the night and never heard from again. No one was safe, for no one could be trusted.

Fearing the actions of the underground and aware that instructions from and news concerning the resistance spread by word of mouth, the occupation authorities had plastered the city with posters saying, *"Roddelen schaadt Uw Volk* (Gossip hurts your people)." They followed it with an edict known as *"Polizei Standrecht"* which forbade gatherings of more than two people on the streets. One day while two women had stopped in front of a store window, another woman paused briefly by them to glance at the same window display. A shot rang out from across the street, killing her instantly.

Because of such ruthless attacks on the innocent, it's no wonder the underground movement evolved into a formidable opponent of

Scholtenshuis, the Gestapo headquarters in Groningen. The sign over the main entrance reads "V Victory because Germany is winning for Europe on all fronts."

the Germans. They were determined to destroy us and our will to resist, and we had to fight back in order to survive.

The stabbing death of a uniformed soldier on a darkened street brought on an early evening, strictly enforced curfew. By this time two new dreaded words entered the Dutch language. The first, *Ausweis,* a German permit, heavily signed and swastika-rubber-stamped, exempted its bearer from officially issued regulations. The Germans knew that thousands of counterfeit *Ausweise* were in circulation, so having one was by itself no guarantee that the authorities would honor it. Instead, any slight irregularity or a smudged rubber stamp could mean a trip to a concentration camp. Naturally everyone, whether guilty or innocent, was terrified at having to present their

A parade of German motorized infantry in front of Groningen's city hall.

Ausweis on demand. *Razzia,* meaning raid, was another word that terrified even the guiltless.

But while the Nazi administration, led by their bespectacled Austrian-born Reichskommissar (State commissioner) and Hitler's highest representative, Arthur Seyss-Inquart (jokingly known by the people as "Six-and-a-quart"), strengthened its stranglehold on the civilians and replaced the former administration with Dutch Nazis and their puppets, I lived for a period of three weeks in a fantasy world of my own. The first load of rifles had been delivered, and so had 100 small brown bakelite Phillips radios that we later distributed to those daring enough to possess one after the Germans had forced everyone in the country to turn in their sets. They were invaluable since the "underground" headquarters in London always broadcast instructions to the resistance movement during BBC or Radio Vrij Nederland

(Radio Free Netherlands) news bulletins.

In my fantasy, I waged my own battle against the oppressor. Several mornings a week after leaving the house for school, I would instead turn left, run to the warehouse, and climb the narrow stairs to the third level, carefully avoiding the upholsterers. Tiptoeing to the corner where a new shipment of chair and couch frames had been stacked to the ceiling, I crawled underneath for about 30 feet until I could touch the three rifle crates. Then I'd lift the lid and slip my hand inside until I could feel a gun. Holding the lid up with my left hand, I reached in with my other hand and pulled the rifle out of the box. After backing out from the stacks, I'd position the gun in front of me by resting it on a frame leg with the barrel pointing to the crack in the door of the loading platform and the street below.

The Austrian-born Arthur von Seyss-Inquart, Hitler's personal governor for the Netherlands. After the war he was tried and hung at the Nürnberg war trials.

The gun was always empty, but it gave me a powerful feeling nevertheless to know that with this weapon I could determine the destiny of a German soldier. From my vantage point, I watched the intersection of our street, the Binnen Damsterdiep and the Korreweg, a major crossing in our part of the city for all traffic coming from the border. Sometimes I'd lie there for several hours until a German staff car crossed my field of vision. Moving the rifle carefully, I'd aim it at the officer's head and squeeze the trigger.

"There's another one for Holland," I said to myself as I watched him crumple over in my imagination.

I wish I could tell my friends about this, I kept thinking, *but I know I can't because no one is supposed to know about the rifles.*

No one in the shop or outside on the street could see the gun barrel. None of the upholsterers knew about my silent war except "Dove," our mute cabinetmaker who assembled furniture frames. Whenever he noticed me lying on the floor, aiming the rifle, and saw my finger pull the trigger, he'd wink, raise his finger, then cut another notch on the edge of his work bench. Even though he couldn't speak, I could read, "Well done, boy" in his eyes. The Germans in my war game, of course, never knew they had been killed, but that did not decrease my satisfaction. After three weeks of silent killing, I was forced to abandon my lonely battle. Falling grades and notes from the teacher to my parents forced me back to school, but by that time my imaginary cemetery was already half full and I was content.

Late one night, just before climbing the ladder to my bedroom, my father stopped me and said, "We're going to move the rifles tomorrow morning."

Without hesitation, I blurted out, "May I come along, Dad?"

Shaking his head, he muttered more to himself than to me, "I can't expose you to that danger. I have to take them out of town—and there may be roadblocks."

He didn't give me any details. It was obvious he was protecting me from such a dangerous job as transporting arms for the resistance, but when sleep finally closed in on me that night, I had made up my mind. I would be there in the morning. When I arrived at the warehouse at 7:00 a.m., Dad was already there with a *bakfiets*. He had decided not to use the small furniture delivery truck this time. When he gave a preoccupied glance in my direction, it was obvious that it hadn't registered that it was a school day and that I shouldn't be there. The crates were already on the way down, swaying gently on the end of the cable and occasionally banging against the brown brick wall. I grabbed the cable as the load reached the sidewalk, and he and I picked up the three crates and laid them on the cargo platform of the tricycle. Seconds later the cable had been hauled up and was already descending with a few old chairs and a couch in need of repair which we placed on the *bakfiets* to hide the crates from view. "You don't really mind if I come along, Dad, do you?"

He thought for a moment, then agreed to my jumping on the couch. We both thought I might make a good decoy. With a child he would be above suspicion, we hoped. With him pedaling we soon reached the Noorderhaven and the Leeuwarde Straatweg. The 20-minute ride was quite uneventful until a German truck careened around the corner of the Kraneweg, a busy side street, and headed straight for us. Bracing myself for a collision, I turned and watched my father. Anticipating the crash, he was already rapidly backpedaling and putting the torpedo brake in action. By that time the heavy load of rifles had slid forward, banging into the front board of the cargo box. I gasped, and it seemed to be several minutes before I was breathing again.

The driver never slowed down but yelled a stream of German curses at us as he passed. Dad started pedaling again over the uneven brick street until it merged with the main tree-lined road leading to Leeuwarden, the capital of Friesland, the neighboring province. The sunny sky under which we had started had now changed to a gloomy gray. The temperature had also dropped noticeably. Looking ahead I suddenly shivered, and it wasn't just from the cold, for I had noticed three black-uniformed men standing quietly behind one of the tall oak trees between the road and the soft green meadow on the right. Dad had seen them too. Turning around to watch him, I noticed his right hand slip into his coat pocket and retrieve the Dutch Nazi party pin Uncle Gijs' friend had given him to use in case of emergency. Quickly sticking it on the lapel of his jacket, with renewed vigor he began pedaling at full speed again.

"We've got a roadblock," he mumbled under his breath as we approached the human barrier.

One of the three — a policeman — stepped to the middle of the road and raised his hand, commanding us to stop. Dad engaged the brake and raised his right arm in the Nazi salute. The two blackshirts also made an appearance with the Dutch Nazi greeting *"Hou zee"* (meaning, hold the right sea course, a natural for a seafaring nation).

The policeman touched Dad's shoulder as we slowly biked past and said, "What do you have on that cart?"

I said a quick prayer.

"I'm taking this furniture to the lady who lives in that house to find out what type of material she wants on them," my father told him.

We had to keep him from reaching under the couch at all costs because discovery of the rifles would mean the Gestapo and Scholtens Huis for our entire family.

Smiling confidently, Dad pedaled on, both of us desperately praying. About 200 meters down the road we turned sharply into Mrs. Tolma's narrow driveway, stopping only when we pulled in behind the horse-drawn manure cart that had pulled in just ahead of us.

The driver jumped off the seat, grinning nervously, as my father walked over to him. "That sure was a narrow escape wasn't it? How did you get past those Nazis? They've stopped and searched everyone who passed their checkpoint for the last 30 minutes. I've been here that long and was thinking about heading in your direction to warn you, but then you came. Have you got the shipment?"

Dad nodded silently.

Grabbing a shovel, the driver began digging a hole in the stinking, brownish mess. We then helped him drag the three crates off the *bakfiets* and onto the cart, shoving them deep inside the manure pile. After covering the crates completely, we felt sure that no one would attempt to search the wagon once it was on the main road. The stench was too overpowering.

With our mission accomplished, we pedaled past the checkpoint again, giving a Nazi salute. We did not allow ourselves to relax until we arrived home safely.

Standing at the sink, Mom turned and smiled nervously as we stepped down into the kitchen. Her men had returned—but little did she know the danger that we had faced. Gunrunning or anything remotely connected with promoting violence had always been completely contrary to our religious beliefs, but we felt that God somehow understood what we were doing now. As conservative Christians we had always relied on God through prayer, and we knew that in one way or another He would see us through this war, as long as we did our share.

CHAPTER THREE

Death Trains

Soon after the occupation began, the Netherlands royal family, consisting of Queen Wilhelmina, Crown Princess Juliana, her husband Prince Bernhard, and their two daughters, Beatrix and Irene, settled in their new quarters in London. Concerned for her daughter's safety, the Queen insisted that Juliana and the children move to Canada for the duration of the war. She, however, remained in England and did whatever possible to maintain and strengthen the royal house's ties with the suffering population of her country, making it her policy to personally receive as many escapees as her schedule permitted. Also she determined to be as well informed about conditions in Holland as humanly possible.

The story is told of the elderly Queen receiving a resistance fighter one wintry afternoon. He looked startled when he entered her door and saw her knitting a woolen sock.

"You look shocked, young man. Are you surprised to see your queen knitting?" With that remark she pulled up the hem of her long skirt to show him the socks that she had just made for herself. "I also knit socks for the needy." After their talk the soldier left the room, convinced that Holland had been blessed with a caring monarch, and that is precisely how Dutch history has recorded her.

Even though Prince Bernhard had been born a member of a princely family in Germany, he assumed the leading roll in the Dutch resistance movement, directing policy and overall operations against the country of his birth and of his brother who was an officer in the German air force. This greatly endeared him to the Dutch people.

One day my father came home with a number of newly arrived photographs of the royal family. Whether the pictures or negatives

The aging Queen Wilhelmina encouraging her occupied nation via the micro-phone of Radio Vrij Nederland (Radio Free Netherlands) from its broadcast studio in London.

had reached Holland by courier or had been dropped by parachute, no one seemed to know. But the demand for them was much greater than the supply. Because of my interest in photography, the underground asked me to print up one thousand copies. It was too risky to have it done through one of the city's photo stores. So, using some parts from an old bellows camera bought at the local flea market, I built my own enlarger and set up shop in a five-foot deep hall closet. For the better part of three weeks, I managed to print 100 copies a night, packing each stack into little wooden cigar boxes for my paternal grandmother to pick up early the following morning. She would then deliver them to a list of addresses known only to her.

It was a nice easy routine that made me feel that I was doing my share to irritate the occupying powers, and one evening during the third week, we found out just how much of an annoyance my pictures had become to the Germans. It was long after curfew, and we were just getting ready to turn in for the night when the loud clanging of our brass doorbell startled us. Next we immediately heard hard knocking on the door. Dad was still pulling the door open when five felt-hatted

The little girl in the center is Princess Beatrix while in exile in Canada. During the starvation winter of 1944-1945 she was heard saying that she wanted to grow up to be a farmer's wife so she could feed the starving children in the Netherlands. She is the country's current queen.

Gestapo agents pushed past him, followed closely by two Dutch stormtroopers. Without asking any questions, they ran from room to room, yanking open every door in the house. They examined each cabinet and closet and pawed through every drawer, scattering our belongings everywhere. Still without a word, one of them opened the door to my darkroom and stood there with a puzzled expression on his face.

Standing in the hallway across from the room, I mentally went over every inch of that room, hoping that I had not been careless enough to leave any incriminating evidence laying about. I had already disassembled the enlarger and hid it and the paper and chemicals under the kitchen trash kept in a container standing in the courtyard. Had I overlooked anything? I felt a shiver running down my spine as I thought about the probable consequences if I had left something out.

Dad quickly rushed over. "That's my boy's hobby room," he explained nervously, showing them a wooden Stuka model airplane. When the officer's glance drifted toward a small stack of wooden cigar boxes on the shelf, my father continued quickly, trying to distract him, "Don't you think it's a good replica of the famous dive bomber?"

I felt totally helpless as I stood staring a hole in the floor.

"Don't let them find anything wrong," I pleaded silently. "Please God, don't let them open the cigar boxes with the negatives. Also don't let them find any *onderduikers* (hidden fugitives) or take us to the Scholtenshuis." The fear of being hauled off to Gestapo headquarters was always there. It never left us. Whenever anyone left home for whatever reason, they'd always pray that they would not end up in the Scholtenshuis. Just because you breathed and were alive in the morning was no guarantee that you would still be around by nightfall.

"There's nothing here! Let's go!" barked the German standing by the darkroom door, and he slowly headed toward the entrance hall. His men followed, and without any explanation of why they had come, they left, slamming the front door behind them. We all seemed to exhale sighs of relief at the same time, and as for me, I wouldn't have been surprised if my hair had turned white. Suddenly I felt much older than my 11 years.

After such an incident, we always looked forward to having friends over to relax, and at some point the conversation would always revert to the history of Groningen and that of our house. Historical records first mention the city in 1006 as belonging to the Triantha tribe. Even today the old part of the city still has its former moat that later became part of a system of picturesque canals. The city was walled in 1255, and in 1536 came under the rule of Charles V. During the great wars of the 16th century it suffered all the miseries of siege and military occupation. In 1580 a treacherous governor handed the city over to the Spanish. It seemed that Groningen was always at war with the surrounding counties and nearby German city states, and in 1672 the Bishop of Munster besieged it, but the city successfully resisted the attack. The population still celebrates the defeat of the Bishop of Munster and Cologne each year with fireworks on August 28, a custom similar to the 4th of July in the United States. Iron cannonballs of that war still lodge in the walls of some of the city's oldest buildings which at that time were located on the outskirts. However, Groningen's inhabitants tore down most of its defensive system of gates, walls, and moats in 1874.

Aside from its distinctive style and it being 320 years old in 1940, we did not attach any special significance to our house's location near the former city wall and gate. But a few years after the war began, we discovered one of it's best concealed secrets. Late one afternoon Dad and I were moving some things in the basement when he accidentally dropped a hammer on the slate floor and we heard an unexpected echo under us. That evening we chiseled a hole into the slate slab and realized that we had forced an entrance into an ancient tunnel leading toward the direction of the location of the former city gate. Once the hole was large enough, dad lowered me into the cavity. With my flashlight I noticed the sides were a combination of brick and cobblestone with stone slabs overhead. Up ahead the floor of the tunnel was wet and it looked as though water from the nearby canal had seeped in over the years, muddying up the bottom. When my flashlight beam caught a few scurrying rats, I was not as brave as I thought I would be and didn't dare to go any further. Instead I yelled to my father to pull me up out of the hole and never went back, although I recollect we once used it to hide someone for a night.

The historical struggles of Groningen which included being ruled by the king of Spain and controlled by the French Republicans from 1795 until 1814, probably led its Dutch nobleman builder to place in it some of the most unique hiding places in all of the city, none of which the enemy ever discovered.

In some places the walls were nearly a foot thick. Over a room measuring 10 by 20 feet that separated the living room from the dining room which had a ceiling 4 feet lower than the other rooms we discovered a large space between the ceiling and the floor above. A large painting halfway up one of the walls of the dining room concealed the entrance to the chamber. If the Gestapo had ever found it, there would have been no end to their frustration, as the narrow opening could never have accommodated their broad shoulders and fat bellies.

After the first few years of the war, I began to regard the secret room as one of my own private hideouts. Outfitted with ample reading material, candles, blankets, some canned food, a bottle of water, and a German gas mask in its original blue-gray metal case, anyone could have stayed hidden there for several days, or even longer if necessary. During all of their raids, the Gestapo never once moved the painting.

The house in the center right was the author's home during the war years. It was built in 1620, and this photograph was taken just prior to May 1940.

There was even a latched door on the other end of that room which led into the apartment of the Nazi family upstairs, which had a separate entrance next to the main house. There was no way that the 23-year-old woman who lived there could know or suspect that the little hideaway existed or that I could hear her entertaining her occasional German Army or Navy boyfriends in her bedroom on the other side of the wall. She had lots of men friends who visited her regularly during the war years. Her husband couldn't object, because he was fighting in a Dutch division of the German Waffen SS on the front and was never home.

Soon after my 15th birthday I remember her calling to me from her apartment and asking me to help her move some furniture. Her true motive wasn't apparent until she invited me to sit down. Removing her skirt, she sat on my knees. I had grown up in a conservative Christian family and her behavior shocked me. What made her actions even more repulsive was the fact that she was the enemy—a Nazi. Wanting nothing to do with her, I bolted out of the room.

Not long after I turned 12 in September 1940, the Germans began preparing for a sea invasion of England. They assembled a mighty armada of over 3,000 self-propelled barges in the harbors of Holland, Belgium, and France. Realizing that their own ships were not adequate to transport 11 divisions for the first planned wave of invasion troops, they confiscated anything and everything that would float and carry at least one armed soldier. Hundreds of yachts, small sporting boats, and even canoes were soon tied up at docks and canals all over the region.

"Are they really going to invade England with those boats?" I wondered out loud to my father as we bicycled past a number of moored vessels in a canal.

"Son, there's no way they'll succeed in their attempt to cross the channel," he replied. "That body of water is too rough, but wouldn't it be nice if they did try anyway, because that would mean a lot less Germans to worry about." We both smiled.

German propaganda focused heavily on their invasion threats, and the song we had heard when the thousands of soldiers trooped past our house that first day of war, *"Und Wir Fahren Gegen Engeland,"* became even more popular than ever.

Another major topic of interest on the radio and in the German-controlled newspapers dealt with the Italian attack on Egypt and the Fuhrer's plan for a meeting with the Italian dictator, Mussolini. It finally took place in the fall of 1940 at the picturesque Brenner Pass between Austria and Italy. Both the Fuhrer and El Duce had grand desires to create fascist empires. Hitler's victories against his Western European neighbors was followed in November by an Italian attack on Greece. It was clear to us that the two dictators were trying to outdo each other.

By the end of the summer, long-term German preparations had already begun for the invasion of Russia, and on December 18 Hitler issued his famed Barbarossa directive. It informed his military staff about his plans to crush Soviet Russia with one decisive campaign.

Only Hitler's closest associates had access to all the details of "Operation Barbarossa." In May 1941, just prior to the attack on Russia, Rudolf Hess, the Fuhrer's adjutant, took a fighter plane and headed straight for England. His self-appointed mission was to arrange peace between Hitler and Britain and possibly to furnish the British with details of the plan to move east. However the British thought he was insane and imprisoned him in London. At the Nürnberg Trials he received a life sentence and ended his days in Berlin's Spandau prison as a war criminal.

Toward the end of the first year of occupation, the Allied bombing raids to Bremerhaven and Emden in Germany increased steadily. Lying in bed at night in the dark, I would hear the faint drone of airplane engines in the distance. As the roar of the squadrons got closer to the city, the howling of the air raid sirens sounded, and it was then that I would feel the beginning of an asthma attack. I had been suffering from asthma since early childhood, but the fear brought on by the nightly overflights brought on the severest attacks.

My parents soon realized that my asthma medication was not strong enough, and Dad applied for and received an *ausweis* to allow him to be outside at night to either summon a physician or pick up medication at the apothecary a block away.

After an especially acute attack one evening, my parents summoned the doctor, and as part of his treatment he had me run around the block with him. I didn't think I would make the first 100 feet, but surprisingly, my breathing got easier.

Once as the two of us ran during curfew with the brilliant beams of searchlights crisscrossing the black sky overhead, a nervous sentry challenged and almost shot us. Only after Dr. Vaandrager identified himself and explained the reason for our being outside did he allow us to continue jogging toward home. It was an unorthodox and dangerous treatment, but it worked!

Hitler's hatred for the Jews hit Holland full force in late 1940 when the occupation authorities ordered all Jews to register and wear six-pointed yellow cloth stars with the Dutch word "Jood" embroidered on it. They had to sew the stars on coats, jackets, dresses, and sweaters. A Jew could not go outside of his home without the yellow star. To do so meant a quick trip to a concentration camp.

The new ruling immediately affected our family. Stina, my father's youngest sister, had married Max Israels, a Jew. Even though he was married to a Christian, he still had to wear the infamous star, but because of his marriage the Germans allowed him to stay home a few months longer after the mass deportation started. It gave him a little more time to make plans to go underground. Considering himself more of a Christian than a Jew, he became extremely self-conscious about his star of David.

It was about this time that the Nazi officials of the housing administration began visiting the larger houses on our street, scouting out available quarters for the German officers and non coms connected with their motorpool next door to our warehouse and upholstery shop. Quickly they commandeered our main living room at the front of the house for a German soldier named Paul Dirksen and later his wife. Paul, a sergeant who came from the German city of Emden just across the border from our province, disapproved strongly of Hitler's methods. However, his wife more than compensated for his lack of fanaticism.

Although we at first reluctantly accepted our new boarders, soon their presence proved to be a definite advantage. After overhearing conversations between Paul and his wife about battle news and troop movements, my father passed the valuable information on to his brother, Gijs, who would then transmit it to England and the organized resistance.

One afternoon as Max entered the house he encountered Paul in the hallway just about to leave. Sergeant Dirksen stretched out his hand to my uncle who shook his head and pointed to the bright yellow star on his coat. A look of understanding flashed across Paul's broad face, and grabbing Max's hand in a firm shake, he smilingly said, "*macht nichts* (it doesn't matter)" in the low German dialect of northern Germany.

That not every German felt that way was obvious a few months later in early February 1941 when the occupation authorities ordered that all Jews report to the main railway station in each city throughout the country. There they would depart for concentration camps. It tore us apart to see hundreds of families carrying crying babies and pulling young school-age children along. Behind them slowly followed long-bearded orthodox patriarchs, lugging their heavy suitcases as if in a daze. Many townspeople bicycled to the train station to see them off. Every major city in the country had a large Jewish population, including Groningen, and we all cried—not because Jews were being carried off to camps, but because the occupation authorities were forcefully taking thousands of Dutch nationals away from us. That they were imprisoned for being Jewish was not as important to us as the fact that they were Dutch and our friends.

I recall my mother going to the station to say goodbye to the Valks, a Jewish family who had recently joined our church. They had six children ranging from a tiny baby to teenagers, and as my mother watched Mrs. Valk board a cattle wagon clutching her infant girl in her arms, she wept.

We knew from radio reports of Hitler's invasion of Poland how he had mistreated the Jewish population there, and it was obvious that those who boarded the trains that day in Groningen would probably never return.

What the Germans were doing shocked the whole nation, especially the personnel of the Dutch national railroad who transformed their outrage into action. Engineers as well as other essential workers refused to man and run the trains waiting to transport the Jews out of Holland. In retaliation the Germans lined up several hundred railroad employees and others who had attempted to block the deportation, and brutally shot them. Today you will still find plaques on buildings in many cities listing the names of those murdered for listening to their conscience. Many Christians filed into their churches that day to pray for the protection of the deportees while the trains—now manned by Dutch Nazi engineers—pulled out of the stations.

Before reporting to the railroad stations, many Jews asked their

Gentile acquaintances to help hide some of their belongings until the end of the war. That way they would have something to come home to should they survive the concentration camps. The Germans had already announced that anyone caught concealing Jewish possessions would suffer the same punishment as the Jew who owned them.

The day before leaving for Germany, one of our business acquaintances asked my father to hide all of his family's shoes. Without hesitation, Dad agreed and secreted the crate somewhere deep within the clutter of the warehouse. Sadly enough, our friend did not return to claim his things after the war, and one day, shortly after the liberation in 1945, Dad and I climbed the narrow steps to the top floor of the warehouse to look at the box. To our astonishment, we saw that the man had filled the entire crate with 100 left shoes. We had risked our lives for them while someone else had obviously done the same for 100 right ones.

Not every Jew meekly boarded the trains. Several hundred in Groningen joined the others who were already in hiding from the Gestapo. We knew that it was only a matter of time until the Gestapo summoned Uncle Max. They would never overlook him just because he had married a Gentile. Also we realized that it would be extremely difficult to find a hiding place for him for the duration of the war. After all, no one could predict how long it would last, and the population was becoming extremely cautious.

Every day we heard stories about Jews being caught and revealing the names of the families that had protected them, hoping that by cooperating with their captors, they would receive a lighter punishment. Unfortunately, they wound up in the camps anyway along with those who had sheltered them.

Max's orders to report to the railroad station arrived a few months later in June 1941. Although reluctant to leave the country because of his wife, he saw only two options—board the train or be shot. From Groningen the Germans sent him to a small transit camp in Westerbork in northern Holland to remain there until enough prisoners had assembled to warrant transportation to a major concentration camp in Germany. Westerbork was the same camp through which Anne

Westerbork transit camp for Jews and captured fugitives.

Frank passed on the way to her death in Bergen-Belsen.

The uncertainty and fear about Max's fate caused Stina's already severe heart condition to worsen, and concerned for the life of his youngest sister, my dad began to formulate plans to free Max. Any day the camp would ship its prisoners to Dachau, Bergen-Belsen, Auschwitz, or any of the other 19 extermination camps, and his brother-in-law would be lost forever.

Bribing the head of the nearby German Army motorpool, dad secured a military staff car together with a uniformed driver, and an hour later walked with an arrogant swagger into the office of the camp commander of Westerbork. Displaying his Nazi swastika pin on the lapel of his suit coat, he saluted the commandant with a swift *Heil Hitler* greeting. After exchanging a few remarks about the troublesome Jewish prisoners, he said casually, "I am from the Groningen office. I am here to see prisoner Max Israels. Can you get him for me?

Jewish prisoners at work in one of the barracks of Westerbork. Here Anne Frank waited until her shipment to Germany, and from here the author's father tried to rescue his Jewish brother-in-law.

We need to interrogate him again in Groningen."

A few quick commands and five minutes later, Max, followed by two guards, walked through the doorway. He showed no sign of recognition when he confronted my father posing as a member of the Gestapo. Walking into an adjoining room, Dad, in a low voice, instructed Max what to do.

"Stay close to me when I walk out of the office," he whispered. "Walk with me to the staff car outside, and we will drive out of here together. The commandant knows I need to talk to you and that I am taking you back to Groningen." As they started out the door, my father sent up a prayer that his plan would work without a hitch. Unfortunately, he hadn't counted on his brother-in-law losing his nerve. As they approached the gate, Max turned without a word and headed back to his barracks. My father had no choice but to pretend that he no longer needed his prisoner. Angry that he had risked his life to free his brother-in-law but understanding Max's fear, Dad returned to Groningen without him.

Stina was in tears after my father explained what had happened, but two days later we learned to our astonishment that Max had actually escaped and was safely hiding out in the city. It was my grandmother who told us the news.

"Max is back," she blurted out as she entered the house. "He's escaped from Westerbork and is hiding in a house a few kilometers away."

It took three days before we could rendezvous with him and hear his harrowing tale.

"A few Germans, aided by two trustees, were repairing the barbed wire fence at the camp," he told us, "and when they left for a few minutes to get some more supplies, I crawled though the strands of wire. The barbs cut right through my jacket and shirt," he complained, and pulling his shirt out of his trousers, he showed us the deep, bloodied scratches on his back.

"It was late afternoon," he continued, "and I walked a while until I began hearing loud German voices and the barking of guard dogs closing in on me. I crawled into the nearest *sloot* (a shallow irrigation ditch separating the fields) and lay perfectly still in the water until the sounds faded. I guess the dogs lost my scent and headed back to camp."

"What happened next, Uncle Max?" I interrupted excitedly. "Where did you go from there?"

"Well, it was dark when I crawled up out of the *sloot*. I didn't dare to stand up, so I just crawled along on my stomach through the meadow until I noticed the lights of a house in the distance. As I approached closer, I saw that all the lights on the first floor were lit and shining brightly outside, something strictly forbidden under blackout regulations, but at that point, I was too tired to question why.

"Desperate for help and hungry, I decided to take my chances, and standing up, I walked to the back door and knocked softly at first, then louder when there was no reply."

"Who lived there, Uncle Max?" I jumped up and moved my chair closer to catch every detail.

"Settle down, Rene," I heard my father say. "Let him finish his story."

"Suddenly the door was yanked open and a man appeared in the opening. His eyes scanned me quickly from my head to my soggy trousers. He couldn't have avoided seeing the yellow star and my torn jacket. Being that close to the Westerbork camp, it was obvious that I was an escaped prisoner. But his arm shot out, grabbed me by the shoulder, and pulled me inside the house. A few feet into the narrow hallway he opened a door and shoved me headlong down a short stairway into the cellar.

"That's about all I remember until I awoke the next morning," Max went on. "The man I had seen in the doorway brought me some food and explained that he was the local mayor and last night had been entertaining the camp commander upstairs in his living room. He apologized for the rough treatment. I knew now he was just trying to protect me, but the night before laying on that stone floor, I had thought, 'I'm a dead man!'

"After arranging with a farmer to hide me in his cart, he had me taken to another destination and then smuggled into Groningen. I'm just glad to be alive."

We were all happy to have him back, but the subject everyone now discussed was Hitler's invasion of Russia on June 22, 1941, a day before the anniversary of Napoleon's ill-fated invasion. Hitler deployed 150 divisions, most of them armored. The Germans attacked with a 3-million-man invasion force against 2-million Russian troops along a battle-line stretching 2,000 miles from the Arctic to the Black Sea. We could not imagine the Germans being able to defeat the Russian army and endure the harsh winter as well. But so certain were they of quick victory, the German leadership did not even issue its soldiers winter uniforms. We all thought that Hitler should have taken a lesson from Napoleon and left the Russians alone.

By mid-July the Germans had advanced to within 200 miles of Moscow, only to wait until October 2 to march any further. By now the troops were tired and discouraged, and the country was a morass as the weather worsened. During the first week of December the Germans launched another effort and some troops even penetrated into the suburbs of Moscow, but for the most part they were held up in the forests surrounding the capital.

For weeks the joyful news of Hitler's folly was on everyone's lips. Dad was overjoyed at the thought that the German Army would be defeated in Russia. Of that he had no doubt! The end of the war seemed imminent, and one of our close friends even threw a victory party when the news of Hitler's move east became known. Then we heard of Japan's December 7 attack on Pearl Harbor two days after it happened via the BBC and Radio Vrij Nederland. Another bulletin soon informed us that Germany and Italy had also declared war on the United States.

"This is the best thing that could have happened for us," I overheard my father say to the upholsterers. "This means the United States will eventually defeat Japan as well as Germany and Italy. It'll be over soon," he said excitedly. "I'm sure it will be over soon."

But his enthusiasm was premature for we would have to endure another three torturous years of war.

CHAPTER FOUR

Masquerades and Razzias

Uncle Ginus, a sergeant in the Dutch army at the time of its surrender, had received orders to report to the occupying forces. The choice of remaining free within the vicinity of his family or confinement in a German prisoner-of-war camp was an easy one to make. He decided to go into hiding—not in somebody's attic or back room, but disguised as a woman of the streets complete with female attire, heavy make-up, earrings, silk stockings, high heels, and dainty underwear. And, of course, counterfeit identity papers. Most members of the family, including his own children, were not aware of his disguise. While they knew that he had gone "underground" to avoid capture, only his wife Annie and a few close relatives realized his new identity.

His disguise was so successful that even friends who had known him for years had a difficult time believing it was Ginus Bakema and not a prostitute until he greeted them in his normal male voice. Only with his closest friends did he lower his falsetto voice and drop his female mannerisms, but because he looked so much like a streetwalker plying her trade, they were always apprehensive and cast uneasy glances up and down the street, hoping their wives would not see them conversing with "that kind of woman!" They probably would have preferred facing an angry German instead of their suspicious wives.

Tall and slender, Ginus stood out among the prostitutes with whom he associated, but his disguise worked, for who would suspect a tough army sergeant to pose as one of "them"? The occupation authorities, however, had not forgotten his existence nor the fact that he was an electronics engineer and that his family still lived on the premises of his electronics store. It made them a frequent target of the Gestapo, who raided them often and unexpectedly, announcing their presence with a kick against the door and bursting into the family's private quarters.

Their surprise searches never caught Ginus, but one day they almost snared Uncle Max who was visiting Annie when they arrived. For more than an hour two Gestapo agents sat on a couch in the living room, facing the door that opened into the hallway and hoping to catch Ginus coming home for a visit. They could not help but notice several long dark winter overcoats hanging from a coatrack in the hall and underneath two pairs of ladies slippers, a few high-heeled shoes, and one lone pair of men's black shoes.

When their expected prey didn't arrive, they disgustedly stubbed out their cigars and headed for the front door. A few minutes after the door slammed, the black shoes began to move and out from behind the coats stepped a shaking Uncle Max. "I thought they would never leave," he trembled. "I was terrified that I might have to cough or sneeze and give myself away." When he and my Aunt Annie heard the kick at the doors, there had not been enough time for him to escape, and the coatrack was his only hiding place. All the while the Gestapo had been looking in the empty hallway facing the coatrack, Max had been standing there, praying that they would not notice any movement behind the coats or possibly a part of his trousers showing underneath. Had he been detected, he knew they would have shot him instantly and transported Annie and her children to a concentration camp for harboring a Jew. After waiting another 15 minutes until he was certain the danger had passed, he left.

It took quite a while before I became aware of what had happened to my uncle Ginus although I noticed he was never there when I visited my favorite aunt. He had simply disappeared. Eventually I overheard a conversation between two of my other aunts that he had become an *onderduiker* and was in hiding. Finally I understood what had happened. However, nothing could have prepared me for the shock when he stood at our door one evening just before curfew. Only a few minutes before his arrival, Flip, a young Jew-on-the-run, had walked in, and I recall that within minutes my parents were embroiled in a heated discussion about where to put him. In my dad's opinion, the house could always hide one more fugitive. Mom was more cautious. We didn't regard Flip as a Jew, but just a Dutch citizen seeking refuge.

While my parents were arguing, I had retreated to my secret hideaway behind the painting to read. Suddenly there came a soft, quick knock on the front door, and moments later the doorknob to the dining room turned and a familiar voice announced the sudden arrival of Uncle Ginus. Looking down into the room through a crack in the door, I thought my eyes were playing tricks with me! For what I was seeing was a neatly attired woman with short curly hair, but what I was hearing was definitely my Uncle Ginus. Was I ever confused!

"What are you doing here at this hour, Ginus," Dad said somewhat irritatedly. "You're exposing us to unnecessary danger. I think that we're under constant surveillance, and his coming here," pointing at Flip, "may signal a *Razzia* at any moment."

"I need help even more than he does!" Uncle Ginus jerked his head in the direction of the young Jew. "I've been walking the streets like this for a long time. You know that!" The more he complained, the higher his voice became until he really began to sound like the woman he portrayed.

By now, my mother had joined the conversation. "Do you really have to look like that, Ginus?" she asked, staring in disgust at his exaggerated makeup and women's clothing. We were a very conservative Christian family, and to see him disguised as a prostitute really upset her. She was ready for anything, but not that!

Dad turned his attention again to Flip. "I'd better first find a place to hide you for the night," he suggested. "Come with me," and grabbing Flip by the arm, he pulled him in the direction of the hallway. "We will house you in the granary for the night. Here's a flashlight. Let's first go into the kitchen and get you something to eat!"

"You mean I can't stay in the house tonight," he retorted, then glanced at Ginus. "And he can?"

"Be reasonable, Flip," my dad answered. "He is my sister's husband. He's family, and besides, since the beginning of the war he's been living the life of a streetwalker, always afraid of being found out. Don't you think he would like to sleep restfully for one night? You haven't been an *onderduiker* as long as he has!"

My mother looked distraught as she walked up to Ginus and put her arm around him. She had always liked him. "I knew you lived like this," she said softly. "Annie told us. But don't worry, we'll find a place for you here." Shaking nervously, she added, "That means we'll have four *onderduikers* under our roof tonight."

At those words, the tough army sergeant in Ginus rose to the surface. "It isn't curfew time yet, and I can still make it to those friends of mine where I stayed last night . . ." Reaching for a makeup kit in his purse, he repaired the smudged makeup on his cheek where my mother had kissed him, and left.

No more than 15 minutes had passed and Flip had just crawled through the small window into the granary, when the brass doorbell sounded, followed by a hard knock and the demanding words *"Öffnen Sie die Tür!"* Scrambling quickly out of my secret room, I slid down the walls, holding onto the bottom of the opening as long as I could, then let go. Four civilians followed my father into the room.

"Where is everyone?" the stockiest and shortest of them shouted.

My mother, acting her part beautifully, dropped the embroidery she was working on in her lap and spoke quietly, "What do you want this time?" In her halting German she continued, "Why do you always come on Friday nights? We have done nothing." She was disturbed because Friday night was always the time when we as a family studied our weekly Bible lesson.

"Let us have your identification cards, *bitte* (please)," one of the four asked, speaking more softly than his chief. After giving them a cursory glance, without another word they filed out the door to the living room. We could hear them pulling drawers open and dumping their contents on the floor. Dad and I followed, both having the same thought: *Did we pull the blackout curtains over far enough to prevent light from escaping to the outside, and did we close the inside shutters?* I shivered. Both windows had black blinds rolled down their full length, and covering them were window length, tightly-latched wooden shutters. When shut, not even a sliver of light could escape, nor was anyone able to see in. The beams of the Gestapo flashlights played about the darkened room like the searchlights crisscrossing in the pitch-black sky outside.

They were looking for any signs of irregularities, such as an unusual crack in the wallpaper or an extension cord disappearing into a hole in the walls, or maybe a door that should not be there. One beam roamed searchingly along the cabinets underneath the unusually wide window sills, *"Was giebt es da?* (What is that there?)" a portly Gestapo agent questioned, almost hissing the words into my dad's face. With the flashlight beam still resting on the door of one of the cabinets, he reached out and opened it. The light began to probe the inside to discover its contents. "Wine?" he laughed heartily. Laying the light on the floor and kneeling down, he grabbed a bottle and pulled out the cork with his front teeth. Then, spitting it out, he stood up, leaned back, and tipped the bottle to his eager lips. His first big gulp was followed by an equally quick gasp.

"Help me!" he wheezed, "I'm poisoned!" He thrashed wildly about the room with the liquid dripping out from between his lips and down his chin. Spewing the remainder of his mouthful over the living room rug, he screamed, "You tried to poison me!" and spat at my father. By now his fellow officers were slapping him on the back, ridiculing his attempt to drink from a bottle without examining and smelling it first. Did he actually think that we had been trying to poison him? It was ludicrous to even imagine we would attempt such a thing in the presence of three Gestapo witnesses. But we didn't dare show any reaction because the situation was too precarious. However, inwardly we were roaring with laughter because he certainly was a comical sight to behold. Obviously, the 24 homemade bottles of grape juice we had stored there had become vinegar. Backing out of the room, we caught one of the other men carefully checking the floor beneath the coal burning stove in the dining room. Fortunately, he did not pull at the stove, for a sideways swing would have revealed a trapdoor beneath that led to a quick getaway route to the cellar and from there to the coalyard and the alley next door.

Once again God had answered our quick prayers to Him. Living as we did in constant danger, we knew we had to survive by a combination of our own resourcefulness and our dependence on God for guidance and safety. Without Him protecting us and the hope that one day we would escape this living nightmare, none of us would have made it.

But it wasn't just the raids that endangered our personal freedom. Expecting an eventual Allied invasion, the Germans had established a construction corps known as Organization Todt to supply able-bodied men to build coastal fortifications and man the armament factories in the Fatherland. The task of recruiting the necessary men from the occupied Western European countries fell to Fritz Sauckel, a former German provincial party leader, who, as a former sailor and factory worker, the German High Command had considered to have the right qualifications to become the master dealer in people. Promising good working conditions, good pay, and paid vacations, Sauckel began his recruitment drive in the Netherlands. The few men who volunteered soon discovered that the promises were broken even faster than they were made. I remember hearing that every man in the city had received an "invitation" to work in Germany. When my father checked around, someone who had actually "volunteered" and was home on leave informed him that "If you tell them you need special food because you can't chew whatever they feed you out there, you won't have to go." Dad listened carefully and began taking measures of his own to assure that he would be exempt from going.

I recall him telling my mother one evening that he would be going to the university hospital the next day to have all his teeth extracted. "This way," he explained, "the *moffen* will see that I'm useless because I'll be unable to eat normal food, and hopefully they won't want to bother with me."

Early the next morning he courageously mounted his bicycle and headed for the hospital, only to return some time later that day holding a small, rattling paper sack in his left hand. I remember seeing him open the bag and spread his teeth out on the table. They had all been pulled in one sitting. I can well imagine the pain he must have endured, for the authorities would not permit the use of anesthetics for mere tooth extractions as they had reserved all available pain-killing drugs for the soldiers at the front. A day or so later dad carried his bag of teeth to the local registration office for labor in Germany and again poured his teeth out of the sack, but this time on the desk of a startled registration clerk. "Here are my teeth. Take these to Germany instead of me," he mumbled. "I had to have all my teeth pulled, and even though I want to go, you can't use me because I won't be able to eat your food."

His plan worked. As far as his labor problems were concerned, the Germans never bothered him again. But because of various evasion techniques the Dutch men used and personal sacrifices such as that of my father, it was impossible for Sauckel to meet his manpower quota in the Netherlands. Thus, instead of relying on volunteers, Sauckel now staged mass arrests and street-side conscription in the country's major cities. He was able to corral several thousand in my hometown alone, but in Rotterdam, a city whose population was still suffering from the aftereffects of the German mass bombing during the early days of the war, his raids bagged him a total of 50,000 men for forced labor. They were just a small part of almost 500,000 of my countrymen compelled to work on the Atlantic Wall coastal fortifications along the channel coast and also in German armament plants.

In France, Sauckel also grabbed thousands of men to work in Germany. Dr. Wilhelm Jaeger, a physician for the Krupp armament factories near Essen, confessed that the French laborers lived under inhuman conditions in the camps. He admitted that "many of them were kept for half a year in dog kennels, urinals, and old baking houses. The dog kennels were three feet high and nine feet long, and the laborers had to crawl into them. There was no water in the camp." My dad, who at 42 sacrificed his teeth to remain with his family, suffered for the remainder of his life with shrinking gums, necessitating a great number of sets of false teeth until his death in 1983. But to him it was worth it!

To stay alive under the German occupation had now become a desperate struggle. Things we had previously taken for granted underwent drastic modifications. Rubber bicycle tires were unavailable, and we had to resort to cutting old rubber hoses in tire lengths and stapling the ends together with bailing wire. It did not provide a cushioned ride but kept us from riding on the bare steel rims of the wheels. The looks of the few remaining trucks and buses also changed. The scarcity of gasoline had made it necessary to run them on "woodgas." I recall seeing huge cylindrical wood burning stoves, in appearance resembling American electric or gas water heaters, mounted on the rear of the vehicles or on separate two-wheeled trailers. The gases produced by the smoldering wood kept the engines running—not efficiently, but they ran nevertheless.

One of the few civilian cars still operating in the city of Groningen during the war years. The contraption visible on the two-wheeled trailer is a wood burner that supplied gas for the engine to run on.

The scarcity of consumer goods made it necessary for us to return to the age-old barter system. Many store owners converted their premises to barter stores to accommodate the demand for goods without the use of money. What was unnecessary and obsolete for one was a treasure to another. Since our "eastern neighbors" had acquired most of the cattle, leather too had become scarce, but luckily we were able to buy shoes with wooden soles. They served the purpose but were uncomfortable and clattered loudly on the pavement. To the people on the farms, the leather shortage did not made much difference as they were accustomed to wearing wooden shoes anyway.

The underground news bulletins printed by courageous members of the resistance movement kept us informed of the Allied victories as well as German losses. So we learned that in May 1942 Field Marshal Rommel and his Afrika Korps, assisted by Mussolini's troops, had captured Tobruk in Libya, then moved on toward Egypt. But faced with a shortage of supplies and fierce British resistance, Rommel found himself stopped a few months later at El Alamein in Egypt. Then, catching the German High Command completely by surprise, Lt. Gen. Dwight Eisenhower, using an Allied force of 500 troop and supply ships escorted by more than 350 warships, landed his men on the coast of Algeria and Morocco in early November 1942. While U.S. troops pushed eastward across Algeria, the British Eighth Army advanced into southern Tunisia. On May 12, 1943, the last organized Axis army force in Africa would surrender. Control of North Africa ended the threat to the British oil reserves in the Middle East, and the situation began to look bad for Hitler's Third Reich.

His shortages were not only of manpower but also of raw materials and consumer goods. Just how critical the situation had really become we learned one day when trucks began roaming the streets with blaring loudspeakers telling everyone to surrender all of their brass and copper for the Fatherland. Soon trainloads of confiscated brass lamps and pots rattled their way into Germany where factories converted them into shell casings. We, too, surrendered some of our brass and copperware just to avoid a house search, for had they subjected our premises to a thorough probing, they might have found worse! The rest of our brass and copper we buried in a tin-foil-sealed plywood tea crate in the pasture of a friendly farmer. Even though the authorities threatened severe punishment to anyone who refused to cooperate, we decided to take the risk anyway and add it to all the other chances we were already taking. We wanted to do anything no matter how trivial to hamper Germany's war effort.

I recall hearing the story of a farm family living far in the province who had buried their brass in a field as had many others. The collection truck roared onto their property one day and the men jumped off, shouting at the farm couple to hand over their contribution for the war effort. When they answered, "We don't have any!" one of the stormtroopers smilingly asked the couple's young son. "Tell me, where did your daddy bury the brass lamps and pots?" Proud to be able to assist the visitors, he innocently took the man by the hand and directed him to a freshly excavated patch of soil around the corner of the barn. A quick dig in the loosened dirt revealed a small collection of copper and brassware. Suddenly a shot rang out, and as the truck drove off, the parents discovered the bloody body of their little boy who had been murdered as punishment for their lie.

Despite the wartime conditions that robbed me of so much of my childhood, I still looked for as many ways as possible to live a normal existence. One attempt involved roller skating on the asphalt streets of the city. Groups of us roamed the inner city streets, weaving in and out of the lanes of cars and bicycles, usually a few feet ahead of pursuing bicycle police who, of course, never approved of us in the traffic. To us teenagers, getting together to skate several times a week provided an excellent opportunity to exchange ideas on how to harass the occupation forces and the blue-uniformed *Jeugdstorm* (Youthstorm, the Dutch Nazi youth organization and equivalent of Germany's Hitler *Jugend)* whose members would invariably summon the police when they saw us careening around the bikes and other vehicles on our skates. They apparently regarded themselves as junior guardians of law and order. Getting even with them and their elders who made up the W.A., the Dutch Nazi Party stormtroopers and law-enforcing arm of the Gestapo, became important to all of us, young and old alike.

At the age of 14, when many of my American counterparts were playing baseball or hanging around the nearby drugstore playing the jukebox, I was spending countless hours in my darkroom/hobby room poring over the pages of a book entitled *Chemistry Experiments That Succeed*. It taught me to how to make magnesium bombs and even produce a bottle of chlorine gas. To pester the Germans, I'd place the magnesium bombs/flares on busy street corners just before evening curfew time, then light a long fuse and walk home. The sudden brilliant white light that illuminated the street corner shortly thereafter would invariably bring the W.A. to the scene to investigate. After all it could have been a magnesium flare dropped by an Allied plane to facilitate a paratrooper drop!

My only attempt at making chlorine gas almost boomeranged. Secluded in my closed room behind a German gas mask, using my favorite chemistry book as guide, I began experimenting with chlorine gas, a greenish-yellow liquid that becomes a poisonous gas when exposed to the air. Unaware that it was seeping out under the door, I suddenly heard running footsteps in the hallway and coughing and retching. Peeking out of the door opening, I saw my mother and sister leaning against the opposite wall and grimacing with pain. "Please stop whatever you're doing in there," they gasped, tears running down their cheeks.

One look at them and I knew what I had to do. Grabbing the one-liter bottle of liquid gas, I charged outside and heaved it as far as I could into the canal in front of the house. It must have been quite a sight to the pedestrians on the street to see me running full speed toward the canal wearing a gas mask and holding a half-filled bottle of liquid in my right hand. I felt badly for my mother and sister because for a few days the effects of the gas caused them much discomfort, but after 14 years of living with me, they weren't surprised at anything I did!

The hostile feelings we harbored toward the W.A. and the *Jeugdstorm* did not include the Hitler *Jugend, the original German Nazi youth group, who in their khaki uniforms often marched down the streets. We didn't like either Dutch organization, but in a way were envious of the German Hitler Jugend because they resembled the outlawed Boy Scouts of which many of us had been members before the war. They at* least belonged to an organization, and we missed that.

Besides the fact that they had their own private school to make them even more unique, we found ourselves envying their uniforms, discipline, and knives. I often passed their school building, as my grandmother lived on a street facing the adjacent park, and we visited her frequently. Anyone could belong to the *Jeugdstorm*, but to become a member of the Hitler *Jugend*, it was necessary to have German ancestry. Because my mother's father, Heinrich Reuter, was a German, born in Stettin in the eastern part of Germany, I was eligible to join the elite group. But even though I admired them in a strange sort of way, they were still the enemy, and when they tried to coerce me into membership two years later on my 16th birthday, they hadn't counted on how fiercely I would resist.

When the Germans outlawed the Boy Scouts and denied me the social contact that organization had provided me, our church youth meetings became even more important. The Seventh-day Adventist Church in Groningen did not have a building of its own in those days, but met in a social hall called Rehobeth in the Jewish section of the city, a block from the Synagogue. The organized youth meetings and a warm home life became the only centers of tranquility in my life. The church sponsored national youth camps in the summer not only kept the young people close to God, but provided an escape for us from the chaotic world in which we found ourselves. Amazingly enough, the authorities of the New Order never voiced any objections to the gatherings, even though the German and Dutch national socialists were decidedly anti-Christian.

Because the 10-day camps never had enough food, the national church union president, Hendrik Eelsing, and my father bought supplies on the black market and had it transported to the camps in a German truck whose drivers had been amply bribed for the occasion. Fervently singing our favorite hymns and youth songs together was a way of giving us all the sense of hope we needed to survive what lay ahead.

Music played a vital part in our lives during the war years. However we were not allowed to criticize the occupying power or compose and sing songs with lyrics that revealed our craving for freedom. Shortly after the invasion a song about the battle of Grebbeberg, near the city of Arnhem where the German panzer (armored) units smashed the concentrated Dutch defenses, became so popular that the occupation authorities soon forbid it. The song told of a mother's only son who lay lifeless on the field of battle because he had defended both his family and his country. Although the Germans would not permit the Dutch to sing the words, the music of the Grebbelied (Grebbesong) took on a new title, "Melodia," and became a favorite selection to play on the horse-drawn barrel organs that performed on the streets throughout the major cities. Its cardboard musical score made to be read by the Dutch barrel organs is among one of my most unique possessions, and time after time that song replays in my mind as I relive those days once again.

When the occupation forces tried to suppress all expression of our yearning to be free, the country experienced a surge of interest in songs that had originated in the concentration camps the British had set up during the Boer War in South Africa. Lord Kitchner, trying to gain control of the gold fields belonging to the Dutch settlers and unable to achieve a quick victory, began imprisoning the wives and children of the Boer soldiers in barbed-wire enclosed camps. The British hoped that would break the spirit of their fierce opponents. The music and lyrics that originated in those camps are hauntingly beautiful and speak of the families' suffering and longing to be free. Therefore it was only natural for the Dutch under German occupation to identify with their poignant words since our entire country was also held captive.

Even though the Nazis spoke out against the songs, they were not able to restrain our singing or our playing them at our youth meetings and at parties at the homes of friends. It wasn't always easy to leave a party because of approaching curfew, and one night I overstayed too long at a friend's house near the army barracks. My father, concerned for my safety, sought the help of our German boarder, Paul Dirkson, and asked that he go after me and escort me home. No one dared to be on the streets during curfew without an *Ausweis*, for immediate imprisonment would be the expected punishment. But with Paul at my side I was safe, for no W.A. member would attempt to arrest me while I was accompanied by a well-armed, bemedaled German sergeant.

Only now do I begin to fully comprehend the important role music played during the occupation. Some of the newscasts originating from Radio Vrij Nederland (Radio Free Netherlands) in London began with the clarinet solo of Gershwin's "Rhapsody in Blue," but the BBC newscasts beamed to Europe always opened with the first few notes of Beethoven's Fifth Symphony played on a timpani, notes that also made the Morse code for the letter "V" as in victory. The tension in a Dutch home as its occupants listened to those newscasts was indescribable. Everyone knew that at any moment the W.A. could kick in the door and arrest them for possession of a radio. Often messages or special instructions to the resistance movement interrupted the newscasts or music, such as "the cows in the meadows are having a good time," or "the waters of the rivers are wet." Another message we often heard was "there will be a happy homecoming." The cryptic messages undoubtedly vexed the Germans and the Dutch Nazis, which of course was part of the resistance organization's plan.

I can still see us sitting around our "forbidden" radio on which we had placed my home-built directional antenna so that we could get a clear signal and avoid the German-generated electronic interference. When not in use, the antenna was always carefully hidden in my secret room or disguised at the beginning of a *Razzia,* as was the radio with its home-built short-wave adapter.

But we weren't the only ones in the family whose lives had become extremely stressful. Uncle Ginus — in a different way — had it even worse. He just couldn't seem to stay out of trouble. One day Dad came home with the news that a German *Razzia* had almost bagged my uncle Ginus while he was walking a shortcut through the city's red light district. While still in his disguise, he had run headlong into a roundup of the city's prostitutes who were being taken to the university hospital for a health check. Apparently the authorities considered them responsible for the sharp rise in venereal disease among the troops stationed in and around the city. When my uncle tried to elbow his way through the line of W.A. and Wehrmacht soldiers, one of them grabbed him by the arm and attempted to shove him into the quarantine truck along with the rest they had already picked up in their unexpected raid. Ginus knew that if he had a physical, the authorities would immediately discover that he was a man and arrest him on the spot. Therefore he had to stay out of that truck at all cost. Suppressing his fright and trying to appear calm, he flirtatiously whispered to a soldier *"Lass mich gehen, bitte, mein Liebchen* (please let me go, honey). Here is my address." Slipping the soldier a piece of paper on which he had written a fictitious address, Uncle Ginus winked coyly and told the German that he was welcome any time.

The soldier fell for the deception, and Ginus survived the ordeal only to find himself soon in another predicament. His wife had recently given birth to a new baby—the result of one of his sporadic visits home. Proud of finally having a daughter, he decided to visit an old friend of the family to brag about the happy event, not knowing that the woman already had a visitor. As he unexpectedly walked into the living room, the friend—caught off guard—introduced Ginus as Mrs. Bakema. Resisting the urge to bolt from the room, Ginus forced himself to join the two women for a cup of tea.

"It's wonderful meeting you, Mrs. Bakema," the other woman smiled pleasantly. "I heard you had a baby recently," mistaking him, of course, for his wife, Annie. "How was the delivery? Was it difficult?"

As Ginus began to squirm in his chair, she continued, "I've been told that it gets harder the older we get. You already have four boys, don't you? To have a girl this time must be really nice. How much did she weigh at birth? You're probably breast-feeding, aren't you?" she rattled on, while glancing at his ample top-half.

Ginus, groping for answers, felt a sudden rush of heat rise to his face and muttered something about how little Mathilda slept through the night now and feeding her was no problem at all. Giggling nervously, he added, "It's nice to have a girl for a change. I was wondering if it would ever happen." Forcing his panic to subside somewhat, he excused himself, pleaded another engagement, and hurried out the door.

CHAPTER FIVE

Narrow Escapes

As I watched through the compartment window as the railroad conductors slowly ran alongside the already moving train, I wondered what new adventure would be starting for me. For several months I had been begging my father to take me to Zaandam, a city close to Amsterdam, to visit my grandfather for the first time. Because of the estrangement between my grandparents, he had not been back to Groningen in many years. My sister had already met him six months earlier while on a trip with my father, and now I felt it was my turn. After I pled my case over and over, he finally consented and agreed to the trip if only to silence my constant pestering.

The British Spitfire fighters had made all long-distance travel quite dangerous. One never knew when they would appear overhead and fire on anything that might be transporting troops or supplies. But after hearing so much about my grandfather from Dad, I was anxious to meet him, and that took precedence over any impending danger.

With two counterfeit *Ausweise* dad managed to secure from the underground, we boarded the train that would take us from Groningen to Zaandam. We had a small cardboard suitcase and a net shopping bag filled with sandwiches and a bottle of lemonade to sustain us for the nearly four hour ride. We more or less ignored the possibility that we might get strafed by Spitfires until at the station we noticed the heavy anti-aircraft guns mounted on a flatbed railroad car coupled at the end of the train. Seeing the ugly black guns manned by their green-helmeted crew made us quite apprehensive, but we decided to chance it anyway. After all, we'd been taking chances since the onset of the war, and we weren't going to stop now. Presenting our *Ausweise* to the W.A. and military checkpoint, we proceeded down the platform and found a half-filled compartment. The Dutch trains have separate compartments, each with its own outside door and windows that one can lower. However, once the train was moving, no one sat facing the wind as minute particles of soot billowing out of the locomotive's smokestack could fly in the window and lodge in the eyes of the passenger.

As the end of the first hour approached, the train began to slow down on the outskirts of a small country town called Beilen. Suddenly the roar of low-flying fighter planes drowned out the rhythmic sound of the wheels clattering on the track. Dad jumped from his seat, and together we lowered the window to see the planes bank sharply and return almost directly into the fire spewed by the train's guns. On their first pass they had completely surprised both the engineer and the gunners. The two Spitfires circled the train again, and with their cannons blazing, began to strafe the train from front to rear. It was the attack that we had anticipated but had hoped would not take place. The dull explosions that followed and the ack-ack sounds coming from the rear of the train indicated that both the Germans as well as our Allied friends were out to destroy each other. After what seemed hours but in reality was probably no more than two minutes, the coaches and freight cars began jolting together as the train slowly squealed to a stop.

The passengers leaped and crawled out of the hurriedly flung open doors and empty window frames, many of them falling into the narrow irrigation ditches between the track and adjacent meadows. The entire scene reminded me of a pan of milk that had been left on the stove too long and was boiling over. I remember seeing one heavyset woman lose most of her dress on the sharp edges of a jagged grenade hole as she tried to squeeze herself out the door of the next compartment. My father and I scrambled out the window and hit the gravel of the track bed as we fell. What had started as a pleasant trip had suddenly turned into desperate chaos. The cursing of the adults, the crying and moaning of the injured, and the gruff German voices, all mingled with the hissing of the disabled locomotive sitting helpless and vulnerable on the track, while at the same time we could hear the staccato firing of the antiaircraft guns at the still circling Spitfires who were now steadily distancing themselves from the train and its deadly guns. In a few minutes we understood the reason for their departure as three German Heinkel or Messerschmitt fighters roared in from the north and Groningen's Eelde airport.

The defeat of the German Sixth army that fought in Russia under the command of the hard-nosed German General Friedrich von Paulus had obviously made the Germans extremely nervous. Any Allied overflight—even by just a few planes—was viewed as a major threat. The decisive Russian victory at Stalingrad against Paulus' 350,000 man army had been highlighted on almost every Allied newscast since his surrender on January 31, 1943. Many historians consider the Battle of Stalingrad as the turning point of World War II. Not only was it the most terrible disaster ever inflicted on a German army in a single operation, but it marked the beginning of the Allied offensive in Europe.

Though bits of information leaked back to us via the radio, we, of course, were not aware that the Allies had already started a massive buildup of men and material on the British Isles in preparation for Operation Overlord, the code name for the invasion of Europe at Normandy under the supreme command of General Eisenhower. Because of their formidable Atlantic Wall fortifications with its concrete bunkers lining the coast all the way from Norway to Spain, Hitler, as well as his commander in chief of the western front, Field Marshal Karl von Rundstedt, were fully confident that the German war machine could successfully fight off any invasion the Allies would attempt. Little did we know that even after the Allies would land on the beaches of France and break through the German lines nineteen days later, we would face the worst period of our lives, the hunger winter of 1944-1945 when several hundred thousand Netherlanders would die from starvation and related atrocities in the southern and western parts of Holland. But that day in the first half of 1943, we were more concerned on how we would get back home.

It was several hours before a few regional buses arrived to transport the shaken passengers back to Groningen where the news of the air attack had already preceded us. Even though it was a frightening experience, no one blamed the British for the damage, because after all, it could have been a troop train. Only those of us aboard it knew any differently. Undoubtedly the presence of the guns on the flatbed were enough reason for the Spitfires to strafe the train. It was just our misfortune to be on it.

I scarcely had time to get over the disappointment of not meeting my grandfather when one morning soon thereafter, Uncle Otto, another of my father's brothers-in-law, stood at our door and whispered to my father that he had a dead German soldier in the back of his horse-drawn milk wagon. Moments after overhearing their conversation, I saw Uncle Otto pick up the body which was rolled in a sheet of canvas and carry it over his shoulder into the alley that led to the back entrance of our basement. The city had not yet awakened to the new day, as it was only 5:30 in the morning, and no pedestrians were on the streets. Because Uncle Otto was a milkman, nobody ever questioned him about being out during the final hours of the nightly curfew. Watching the scene from the kitchen window, I noticed my father quietly step out of the door and grab hold of the soldier's legs.

"Let's keep the uniform clean," I heard my uncle say softly. Fifteen minutes later as I walked down the steps into the basement, I noticed the soldier's nude body stretched out on the stone floor, his bloodied uniform neatly folded beside him.

"I found him in the alley near the dairy with a knife in his back," Uncle Otto explained to my father, "and I thought his uniform would be a nice present for the resistance. Besides, we both know that leaving him there to be found by the police or W.A. would only result in the execution of a number of Groningers as reprisal."

Dad agreed, and both picked up the already stiffening body and rolled it back into the canvas sheet. The milk wagon became a hearse once again.

"I'll dump him into an open septic tank near Hoogkerk where I live," Uncle Otto whispered over his shoulder as he signaled for the horse to move. Only when the sound of the horse's hoofs faded did my father and I breathe audible sighs of relief. We were lucky this time, for had we been caught, our claims of innocence would have been futile and we, along with many others, would have been lined up and shot.

How long would this nightmare go on? Would we ever be liberated? Our spot checks of the war news over the BBC and Radio Free Netherlands had revealed that the tide of war was really beginning to turn against Germany, but it seemed just too good to be true. We were all tired, jittery, and longing for peace.

A few days later Dad and Uncle Otto brought a stunned calf into the side alley the same way they had done the German corpse earlier. The amount of food that the authorities allowed us to buy was never adequate, and my father always kept a vigilant eye for anything that could be traded, talked out of, or borrowed, to ensure that his family would survive and have enough to eat. Three goats tethered in the courtyard supplied us with extra milk and finally meat when they became too old.

Once the two men had the calf in the basement, they slaughtered it and dumped the intestines in a number of galvanized iron buckets. It was my job to cut the entrails into small pieces so one could flush them without obstructing the drain pipes. Using one of our 10-inch long upholstery scissors, I soon had a bucket filled to the brim. Carefully lifting it up, I carried it to another corner of the courtyard to an old outside toilet and disposed of its contents. Obviously, the Nazi woman living on the second floor had no idea what was taking place right under her nose, when, during one of my trips, she opened a window and stared down at me while holding a German Luger pistol in her right hand. It was something she habitually did to intimidate us whenever she saw us below in the courtyard. She knew we had remained loyal to the Queen and the rest of the royal family-in-exile, and, of course, she trusted us no more than we did her.

Clothing as well as food became scarce. One day my father arrived home with a gunnysack filled with freshly shorn wool for my mother to prepare on a spinning wheel that "Dove," one of our cabinetmakers, had constructed for her. Taking turns, one of us would spin wool by the hour, plucking out the large brown ticks before they got woven into the heavy threads. The nimble fingers of my mother and sister, Dina, would magically transform the spools of raw sheep's wool into warm socks and sweaters and sometimes even underwear, which in my opinion caused more itches than warmth. The Netherlands, located on the same latitude as Newfoundland, can be extremely cold in the winter, and woolens are a definite necessity, scratchy or not!

During the war years someone was always dropping by our house to either seek refuge, pass information, or simply enjoy some conversation over a hot cup of tea. One day Professor Weidner, an old friend of the family who lived in The Hague, stopped by. He and my father were both involved in underground activities, and while at our house they discussed finding a new location for a fugitive we had been hiding from the Gestapo for several months. Weidner had quite a sense of humor, and after returning home, sent us a postcard with instructions concerning a new location for the man. Somehow it passed the censors without causing an immediate raid.

The postcard, dated August 1, 1943, said the following:
"Dear brother & family:

"I just received the address of teacher F. S. de Boer, Tramwijk N.Z. 52, Derde Kruisdiep, Niewe Weerdinge, Drente. You know that stamps are very important, don't you? What I took with me from Groningen was a pleasant remembrance. My wife, the daughter of my wife and the father of the daughter of my wife thank you for the way in which you took care of the poor tramp. Your fear that he would get hungry and your worries about their stomachs in The Hague is appreciated. Now I hope that sister [Mrs. Noorbergen] can have some rest, but as long as you don't have a good safe place for the little cat, it will still cause some problems, especially when the doorbell rings. I do hope that a good neighbor will help take care of him. Do let me know. Did you already drill holes in the box so that when you ship it, it will get sufficient oxygen.
We hope for the best.
Greetings.
Give also my regards to my acquaintances and friends."

To us, the wording on the card was almost too obvious, but the

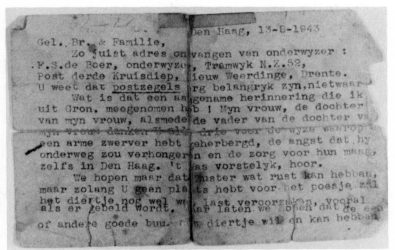

A postcard sent to the author's father giving coded instructions by the father of John Weidner of the Dutch-Paris underground organization.

censors did not take his crazy sense of humor seriously, and it passed their scrutiny without hindrance. However, the reference to the fugitive-in-the-box may have been one of the causes for a raid some time later, and it may have been one of the reasons that we were placed on the *Razzia* hit list again. This we suspected but were never certain. When the card arrived, it was obvious that the stamps had been soaked off, and we still don't know what message they may have concealed, nor to my knowledge did we ever find out if the fugitive we shipped in the crate arrived safely at his destination.

About two weeks later my father decided to give me another chance to meet my grandfather. He obtained a new set of counterfeit *Ausweise* as the old ones had expired. Proudly I walked with him to the main railway station again. There had been no Spitfire attacks since the last one, and we felt quite certain we'd make it this time. Again we passed the checkpoint and were allowed to continue to the platform and board the train. We shared a compartment with two men of approximately my father's age, and within minutes they were discussing the war and the country's economic problems. However, I

Postcard sent by the father of Weidner, subject of the book *Flee the Captor*.

don't recall them dealing with any specific issues, for no one could be trusted in those days, especially strangers. Anybody could be a member of the NSB (the Dutch Nazi Party) or worse.

Because of our previous experience, my father and I sat alert on the bench, looking out the window and listening for the now familiar sound of low-flying planes. If any were in the area, they weren't eager for a fight and stayed out of range of the train and its guns. But trouble of another kind was rapidly approaching in the form of heavy footsteps and Dutch and German voices coming down the narrow corridor connecting the compartments. From what we could hear, they were checking and scrutinizing tickets and *Ausweise*. When the uniformed officials reached our compartment, Dad slipped his hand into his coat pocket and surrendered ours. Their inquisitive glances bounced off the swastika pin he had quickly pinned to the lapel of his coat. Instantly my insides began to feel like jello, and soon my entire body trembled from sheer fright. Since the war had started, Dad for the most part had treated me as an adult, allowing me to witness and take part in some rather dangerous activities, but right now, as I looked into the men's stern faces, I felt like a little boy, and I was scared. As the train ground to a stop, one of the men demanded gruffly, "Let me see your party membership card." Dad couldn't produce one for he was not a Nazi but only carried the pin to use on occasions like this. When they didn't get the expected response, they walked out but returned a short while later with a bald headed civilian. *"Kommen Sie mit* (Come with' me!),*"* he commanded, pointing at my dad. We stood up and followed him down the corridor and out of the train where two other civilians waited to escort us into a small windowless truck.

"Whatever they ask, remember you don't know anything," Dad whispered to me so softly that the civilian sitting opposite us in the truck could not hear. All he noticed was that my father and I were squeezing each other's hand. When the truck stopped in what appeared to be in the middle of a city, he just eyed us and growled, *"Heraus!* (Out!)." The only large city we had passed on the train was Meppel, and the next one down the line was Zwolle.

"Where are we?" I asked Dad, but received no reply. At that point, he wasn't hearing anything.

The canvas in the back of the truck parted, and we stepped out at the edge of a sidewalk running in front of a red brick building, its entrance guarded by two helmeted soldiers. The door was open, and a nod from our civilian escort to the soldiers let us pass. In the hallway we went through more formalities before the soldier at the desk would let the three of us go down the hall. Frisking us, the soldier took our wartime identification cards from our jackets. I was dropped off at what looked like a waiting room. It had only bare walls, a few chairs, and an old desk. The escort took my father further down the hall, where I heard a few more growling voices and then a door slammed in the distance.

Where are we? Why are we here? Why did they take only us off the train? I kept asking myself, but no immediate answers were forthcoming. Hearing quick footsteps passing in the hall throughout the day somehow broke the spasms of fear that engulfed me as I sat there, imagining what they could be doing to my father. *Was this a Gestapo headquarters?* I kept wondering. I asked the same question of a janitor who came to clean the windows and empty the wastepaper basket. The man, looking sad and defeated, listened willingly to my questions, but gave no reply. He just watched me as I sat forlornly, leaning my chair against the window sill. "God, please look after Dad," I prayed silently after the janitor had left and the door closed behind him. "Please make them release him. He hasn't done anything wrong," I continued to plead. God had looked after our family so far, and I just knew He would continue His protection no matter what.

The soft chimes of a church tower clock in the distance was the only way I had of keeping track of the time. I knew it had been close to ten in the morning when the authorities hauled us off the train, and now it was already evening, as the seven strikes from the bell tower indicated. "No word from Dad all day," I mumbled in reply to the seven gongs. I did hear an occasional streetcar (or was it a noisy woodburning truck?) and more heavy footsteps down the hall going nowhere.

Shortly after the clock struck eight that evening, I heard a noise outside my door. Someone inserted a key and pushed the door open and told me to get out. I did, bolting through the opening right into the arms of my father who was standing beside the man holding the key. Dad was fine but looked exhausted. In his hand was an envelope with our I.D. cards, as I found out later. After we left the building, he blurted out, "It was an almost endless interrogation, but I didn't tell them anything. What did they do to you?" But I couldn't answer him, because just then I needed reassurance.

"Did they hurt you?" I questioned worriedly. "This was Gestapo, wasn't it? They didn't torture you?" For an answer, he squeezed my hand, but his eyes were wet as we started walking away. Not knowing where we were and afraid to ask and arouse suspicion, we followed the traffic flow, hoping that it would lead to the main road where we could hitch a ride on a truck or a horse-drawn cart to Groningen. By this time I had decided that if my grandfather and I were ever to meet, he would just have to walk right up to my front door and knock, because I was determined not to attempt to visit him again.

After we had stood beside the road for some time, a farmer hauling a load of hay or straw finally stopped and allowed us to climb on top. Riding as far as Meppel, the last major city we had passed by train that morning, we then transferred to a rattling old freight truck. Fortunately we weren't stopped at a roadblock for we had no reason to be that far away from home. In addition, the slight protection the swastika lapel pin had afforded us in the past was now gone, for "they" had plucked it off Dad's coat before releasing him.

My mother expressed surprise at seeing us return from Zaandam that soon. Her reaction to the enormous stress of the German occupation had been our main concern while in German custody. "How will she take it if something happens to us?" my father and I had discussed briefly before leaving Groningen that morning. Both of us could see the strain really beginning to show on her.

As we were preparing to sit down for dinner one evening soon after our return, we discovered that she had vanished. After searching all the rooms, my sister Dina and I noticed her favorite coat and hat were not hanging in their usual place on the rack in the hallway. Opening the front door to check outside, I saw her standing underneath the lamppost on the corner about 100 feet from our house. Rushing outside, I asked, "Mom, what are you doing here?" She turned toward me, but her eyes showed no recognition. Instead she just looked bewildered and confused.

"I am waiting for Rinke (pronounced Rinka), my husband! Who are you? Go away, boy. Leave me alone!" Soothingly, I replied, "Let's go home, Mom. Rinke is waiting for you there. Everything will be all right."

Our family doctor, whom we summoned later that evening, diagnosed a minor mental breakdown. "This is happening to a lot of people these days," he said, trying to reassure us. "A mild sedative will help for a while, provided you keep as much stress away from her as possible. She can't take much more."

Now more than ever, we wanted the war to end. Our lifeline to freedom, Radio Vrij Nederland, encouraged us daily by the reports of Germany's losses and the conquests of the Allies. We learned that by the middle of 1943, the daily and nightly raids by the Royal Air Force

Identification card issued to the author's mother. The photo shows the emotional strain on her during the war years.

and U.S. bombers were leveling the industrial cities of Germany. Attacks on Berlin also started in the summer of 1943 and continued until the end of the war, totally destroying that city as well. On September 3, the invasion of southern Italy by the British Eighth Army under Field Marshal Bernard Montgomery, had begun. Sailing from Africa, Lt. Gen. Mark Clark's Fifth Army also landed in Italy at Salerno nine days later. Eventually he linked up with the Eighth Army. The drive up through Italy proved to be a slow struggle against a 400,000 German Army led by Field Marshal Albert Kesselring. Pushing to within 75 miles south of Rome by November 1943, the Allies could not seem to pierce the German defenses, and it would take until June of the following year for Rome to finally fall. The end of the war was in sight, but the worst was yet to come!

CHAPTER SIX

From Normandy to Arnhem

I really wonder what is happening out there?" Dad questioned out loud as we sat huddled around the radio to hear the Radio Vrij Nederland news about the Allied invasion. Everyone in the country who dared to possess a radio must have been listening as we were, finding it just as hard to believe as we did that the hoped for invasion had finally begun. The terror and tension the entire country had been living under had intensified to such a level that liberation from the oppressive regime seemed inconceivable, even in the realm of fantasy.

The invasion had been set for June 5, 1944, but because of stormy weather Gen. Dwight Eisenhower, Supreme Commander of the Allied Expeditionary Forces, decided to postpone it one day. Throughout the night of June 5-6 the most intense aerial and naval bombardment of the entire war rained destruction on the German coastal defenses, and parachute and airborne infantry dropped behind the Atlantic Wall to disrupt communications, blow up bridges, and cut railroad lines. Hitler's so-called impregnable fortifications, on which thousands of forced-laborers had worked under deplorable living conditions, were now of little use. Their heavy guns only pointed toward the sea as did the stationery machine guns, making them totally ineffective against the Allied paratroopers who attacked from behind.

For months prior to the invasion, the British Isles had been the scene of intensive training maneuvers. A force of 3 million British, Canadian, and American men had assembled, along with vast quantities of munitions, supplies, and equipment needed for the campaign. The Allies were well prepared with their 5,000 large ships, 4,000

His Royal Highness Prince Bernhard of the Netherlands inspecting the troops of the Dutch Princess Irene Brigade in Normandy during the invasion. He is the father of the current head of state, Queen Beatrix.

smaller landing craft, and more than 11,000 first-line aircraft. "We are about to embark upon a great crusade," Eisenhower told his men before the first wave of infantry began crossing the rough waters of the Channel. They waded ashore at 6:30 a.m. on a 50-mile front along the French coast that had already been softened by a bombardment of up to 200 tons of shells a minute fired from the Allied warships.

I recall reading in a book entitled *Eyewitness to History* an anonymous account by a German soldier in which he described his reaction to the Allied invasion. "On that night of 6 June none of us expected the invasion any more. There was a strong wind, thick cover, and the enemy aircraft had not bothered us more that day than usual. But then—in the night—the air was full of innumerable planes. We thought, 'What are they demolishing tonight?' But then it started. I was at the wireless set myself. One message followed the other. 'Parachutists landed here—gliders reported there,' and finally 'Landing craft approaching.' Some of our guns fired as best they could. In the morning a huge naval force was sighted—that was the last report our advanced observation posts could send us, before they were overwhelmed. And it was the last report we received about the situation. It was no longer possible to get an idea of what was happening. Wireless communications were jammed, the cables cut and our officers had lost grasp of the situation. Infantrymen who were streaming back told us that their positions on the coast had been overrun or that the few bunkers in our sector had either been shot up or blown to pieces.

". . . When we tried to get through to our lines in the evening British paratroops caught us. At first I was rather depressed, of course. I, an old soldier, a prisoner of war after a few hours of invasion. But when I saw the material behind the enemy front, I could only say, 'Old man, how lucky you have been!'

"And when the sun rose the next morning, I saw the invasion fleet lying off the shore. Ship beside ship. And without a break, troops, weapons, tanks, munitions and vehicles were being unloaded in a steady stream."

Of course we had no knowledge of all the details of the invasion, but it was obvious to us that a major military operation was in progress, because after Radio Berlin began broadcasting the news, the German soldiers in Groningen really got the jitters. Trucks and motorcycles roared through the streets, apparently going nowhere, the drivers only stopping to look skyward at the thousands of American B-24 and British Lancaster bombers flying over Groningen on their way to the German harbor cities of Bremerhaven, Emden, and Hamburg. There were so many of them that it looked like an endless flock of giant geese with the tail end of one squadron meeting the beginning of the next. To us, it meant that the German war machine would be dealt another blow, while to the nervous and frightened soldiers, it signaled imminent danger to their families back in Germany. Adding to their frustration over their inability to protect their loved ones at home was

British field marshal Bernard Montgomery in the center and Prince Bernhard on the right, being briefed by a staff officer on the progress of the Allied invasion of Normandy.

seeing the happy smiles on the Dutch civilians as they too watched the swarms of Allied bombers flying overhead. The smell of victory was in the air. We could sense it, and we knew as well as they did that their days were numbered.

Everyone was overjoyed and had a difficult time hiding it. When we received an invitation to an invasion celebration at a friend's house, we accepted happily, knowing we might have to stay over-night, for the evening curfew was still in effect and strictly enforced by the W.A.

But no matter how successful the Allies were at Normandy, Germany was not beaten yet. Disturbing news from London revealed that the enemy had started deploying a new secret weapon known as the V-l, or *Vergetungswaffe* (vengeance weapon), a missile fired from German launching sites along the French coast. The first one hit

London on June 13, exactly one week after the June 6 invasion and would have landed sooner had not the heavy bombing of the area caused a delay in the initial launching date. The Germans launched about 18,000 V-1 or buzz bombs between June 13, 1944, and March 29, 1945.

What no one knew was that Prime Minister Churchill was already planning a revenge of his own to even the score. He had his chiefs of staff draw up a list of major German cities to be bombed with bacteriological agents or poison gas. However, the British never carried through their plan for fear of a new round of retaliation by Germany with the same type of weapon. Berlin, Frankfurt, Achen, Hamburg, and Wilhelmshafen instead faced destruction from regular incendiary bombs.

In the meantime, Allied armored columns closed in on the southern part of Holland. Brussels, the Belgian capital, fell to the British on September 3, followed by Antwerp on the 4th. Soon after this exhilarating news hit the airwaves via the BBC, our Queen Wilhelmina announced that the man we all admired, Prince Bernhard, husband of her daughter, Crown Princess Juliana, had been appointed commander in chief of all Netherlands forces as well as leader of all resistance groups, the latter now to be known as *Binnenlandse Strijdkrachten* (Forces of the Interior). Shortly thereafter, Prince Bernhard's voice came over Radio Vrij Nederland asking that the underground have cloth armlets ready with the word "Orange" on them (the name of the Royal House), but not to use them without his order. He urged restraint, as premature and independent actions would only compromise the Dutch people and the planned military operations.

Then we heard the voice of a friendly stranger, an American called General Eisenhower, who promised, "The hour of liberation the Netherlands have awaited so long is now very near." My sister Dina was not at home that day as my parents and I crowded around the radio in the kitchen, together with three fugitives we were still hiding at that time. We were all ecstatic knowing that peace was at hand, but behind our broad smiles, each one of us was silently hoping we would be able to hold out that long.

Hysterical joy swept the nation, but Seyss-Inquart, the Nazi Reichskommissar for our country, and Anton Mussert, the leader of the Dutch Nazi party, advised all of their followers on September 1 to make plans to leave the country and escape to Germany. They knew the intensity of the hatred their actions had evoked in the country's population and were frightened at the thought of having to face Dutch lynching mobs. Instead they preferred to become prisoners of war of the Allied forces rather than confront the angry Dutch. Seyss-Inquart first headed for his private bunker in Apeldoorn. It was a secure concrete structure with private suites, conference rooms, and a communications center at a location only 15 miles north of Arnhem, not far from the villa that had once housed Kaiser Wilhelm, the German emperor who fled his country to exile in Holland after Germany's defeat in World War I.

Anton Mussert, the Dutch Nazi leader who had always boasted that his party was 50,000 strong, had already entered the panic stage, and he, along with party members and their families, tried to flee the country on the same day, creating chaotic conditions on the roads and in railway stations. They carried bulging suitcases, overloaded shopping bags, and rucksacks, and were a pitiful sight. It is no wonder that this day, September 5, 1944, became known in Dutch history as "*Dolle Dinsdag* (Crazy Tuesday)." However, the German Army and the despised and feared Gestapo still remained to protect the interests of Hitler's Reich. We did not realize at that point that the nation would still have to pay a heavy price for freedom.

I was already looking forward to the day when I no longer would have to eat the homemade sauerkraut we kept in the two-foot-high blue earthenware vat in the cellar, or the dried stickfish. Actually, the latter was dried codfish. In hardness and color resembling a stick, it required extensive soaking and boiling to become edible, that is, if one could ignore its nauseating odor during preparation. We might even be able to buy butter again instead of us having to take turns churning the 25-liter metal container filled with black-market milk. Also, dad sometimes came home with a gunnysack filled with dried leftover bread which he bought from a local baker. By pouring hot milk over it and adding sugar and cinnamon, it became a tasty cereal.

Because the Germans continuously plundered our country, taking food and medical supplies back to Germany, the resulting mass malnutrition caused the elderly to succumb first. Unable to eat proper food and obtain necessary medication for her diabetes, my favorite grandmother (my mother's mother) died in a local hospital on the 25th of September, a day before my 16th birthday. Her death greatly saddened me, for she had always made me feel very special whenever I visited her.

As a small boy I remember getting glasses of water from a little spigot in the kitchen which was attached to a water pipe servicing the rooms on the second floor. It was just low enough for me to reach, and she told me that of all her grandchildren, I was the only one allowed to use it. My mother was her youngest child, and the warm feelings she had toward her "baby" also extended to my sister Dina and me.

Because the local funeral homes were filled to capacity at this time, we placed her casket on two saw horses in the front room that had become vacant when Paul Dirksen had moved out six months or so earlier. Traditionally in Holland, the casket containing the body of a family member is taken from the home to the cemetery after a four-day viewing time, but because of health laws the custom has changed and today the family has its dead taken to funeral homes. Since embalming was not done in Holland, Dad checked my grandmother each day for discoloration and deterioration, and as a sign of mourning, we hung white sheets in the windows facing the street.

That same day, Jan Brinkman, a young ministerial intern whose first assignment was the Groninger district, moved in with us temporarily until he could find a permanent place to live. He was a welcome addition to our household, and I was glad to have him use the guest bed in my room that first night, because I feared having death that close. About 10:00 that evening, as all of us sat around the dining room table discussing the latest war news, the brass doorbell in the hallway began to clang loudly. Usually the first sign of an impending *Razzia*, it would instantly be followed by a hard kick against the door. Dad ran down the hall and opened it.

No one was there. The only one on the street was a German sentry pacing back and forth in front of the granary 50 feet away.

"Did you see anyone ring my doorbell?" he shouted at him.

"Nein!" came the curt reply. *"Ich habe niemand gesehen* (I have not seen anybody.) *Warum fragen Sie das? Es ist Sperrzeit* (Why do you ask? It is curfew)," he added while turning around. Dad muttered something about a prank being played and asked him to be on the lookout so it wouldn't happen again.

Shaking his head in bewilderment, he returned to the dining room, only to hear the bell ring again, this time wildly as if someone was yanking vigorously on the handle. Not only were we frightened, but I am sure the three fugitives in their hiding places between the walls and in my secret room were also trembling. My father and I made another trip to the door, but again saw no one! Walking back down the hall, I felt a sudden chill down my spine as I saw the doorknob of the front room where my grandmother lay slowly turn and the door open by itself.

"Dad, did you see that?" I gasped, pointing to the still opening door. "Please, dad, I'm scared! Let's get out of here!" I said more loudly this time while grabbing his arm and pulling him down the hallway into the dining room. There all of us then began to hear heavy breathing within the room and quick staccato knocks on the walls.

Nothing my father said to reassure me had any effect. I felt uneasy and still scared. Around midnight I awoke to the soft ticking of a clock under my pillow. "Hey, Jan, do you hear that ticking under my pillow?" I whispered loudly to the ministerial intern, hoping he was awake.

Raising up on his elbow, he replied, "I thought it was coming from under my pillow!" His answer frightened me even more.

My eyes had now become accustomed to the dark, and I suddenly noticed the paintings on the opposite wall moving from side to side like colored square pendulums. "Jan, something is wrong here," I continued, whispering, "Let's get out of this room! Now!" Throwing off the blankets was difficult for they had strangely become as heavy as lead. It felt as though I was laying under a steel door with someone pushing down on it. Finally sliding out from under the pressure, I felt a rush of cold air blowing through the room. Checking the window that overlooked the courtyard, I saw that it was securely latched.

My bedroom was in the loft over the kitchen and could be reached by climbing a ladder to a trap door. A wooden railing surrounded the opening to prevent anyone from accidentally falling through it. Jan was already scurrying down the ladder, and I was right behind him at the railing ready to descend when suddenly I felt my legs pulled out from under me, catapulting me down the ladder headfirst. Only by grabbing one of the rungs did I manage to break my fall and prevent my head from hitting the stone tiles in the kitchen below.

What had happened totally mystified me but became a little clearer the following morning after my father mentioned the night's events to our Nazi neighbor. She said something that I have never forgotten. "I made those things happen," she claimed with a laugh, throwing her head back proudly. "I am a spiritualist and have the spirits do those things for me. I know you have a *lijk* (corpse) in your house and wanted to scare you." She had certainly succeeded, and several months went by before I dared to sleep up in my bedroom again.

But her activities did not stop there. A few days later we heard screams coming from her open window and the Dutch words, *"Wij moeten hier weg* (We've got to get out of here)." Dad and I raced out of our house to her front door and were standing there along with the sentry who had also heard the commotion when a hysterical woman and a German sailor flung open the door. Ashen-faced, they excitedly pointed to something behind them in the hallway at the top of the stairs, and without another word, they ran down the sidewalk and out of sight. Baffled at what had just occurred, the three of us stood riveted to the spot looking in the direction the sailor had just indicated. What I saw at the top of the narrow staircase struck terror into my entire being. My knowledge of spiritualism or the power of spirits was quite negligible, but in that one instant I learned a lesson that I would remember my entire lifetime.

Our neighbor hung suspended horizontally in the air, her outstretched arms holding on to the edge of a rectangular dining room table that floated a foot above the floor. Utterly paralyzed with fright, we couldn't believe our eyes. Seeing our bewildered stares, she glanced down and merely laughed. One day soon after the incident, we discovered that she had packed her belongings and vacated her apartment to join the other remaining Nazis fleeing across the border to Germany. We never saw her again.

Because the front line was inching slowly northward, closer to Groningen, my sister Dina, who was taking nurse's training at the nearby university hospital, decided to move home again. Joining her was Fietje (pronounced Feetya) Moes, her roommate, whose parents had been caught in the Dutch East Indies (now Indonesia) when the Japanese overran the islands and were incarcerated in a Japanese prison camp. But along with Fietje came an unwelcome surprise—her boyfriend, a soldier in the Dutch division of the German SS.

Having already fought at the Eastern Front against the Russians, he proudly wore his SS uniform with the skull and crossbones insignia on the cap. Making regular visits to Fietje, he invariably would hear my father say, "You're fighting on the wrong side, Pieter. Some day you'll find out!" At that time we did not know of the atrocities the SS committed throughout the occupied territories as well as in the concentration camps. This did not become common knowledge until after the war had ended.

On September 17, 1944, news came over Radio Vrij Nederland, the BBC, and Radio Berlin, that Allied paratroopers were landing in and around the city of Arnhem about 100 miles southeast of Groningen. That same day Pieter came by and announced that he was on his way to Arnhem to fight the Allied troops. When my dad suggested that now was the right time for him to desert, Pieter refused arrogantly and stomped out, saying, "I can't leave now when the SS really needs me." It was obvious that he had been ensnared by the German propaganda that maintained that Russia was the ultimate danger to Europe, and by fighting alongside the Germans, Pieter, together with many other Dutchmen, felt they were protecting their country from a greater danger than Germany.

The country was delirious with happiness about the Allied landing in Arnhem, but other than praying that the forces would be victorious, the average civilian could not do much to help them. However, another group of my countrymen, the personnel of the national railways, decided to take matters into their own hands and went on strike, refusing to run the troop trains carrying German reinforcements to the battle area. Many paid the ultimate price for their heroic stand when the Germans lined them up against the walls of buildings and executed them. Today, several memorial plaques fastened to the walls of station buildings testify to their courage.

The little reliable battle news that we heard came to us mainly via the BBC. We heard that the British, American, and Polish troops at Arnhem sustained heavy losses from the defending Germans who were fighting for their lives. When the sounds of battle stopped on the 24th of the month, it signaled a decided victory for the Wehrmacht and the SS. The Allies had been defeated.

It was only after the war that I began to hear and read the details of what has become known as "the battle of Arnhem." Dina moved there shortly after the war, giving us many excuses to visit the battleground where the Anglo-American and Polish airborne forces had waged a heroic fight against overwhelming odds for our liberation. Several times since then I have walked among the rows of white grave markers in the Oosterbeek Airborne Cemetery where the sad words, "Known Only Unto God," are the only identification on many small plots of soil. School children adopt grave sites, and each year on the anniversary of the battle, they place their bouquets of flowers on the grass near the plain white markers. The nearby townspeople purposely keep alive the memory of those days, and by having the little ones decorate the graves of the fallen, the sacrifice the soldiers made will never be forgotten.

The area surrounding Arnhem is one of the most beautiful sections in the Netherlands. Rolling hills mingle with fields of heather and thick forests, and it is still hard to believe that it was once the scene of one of the bloodiest battles of World War II.

It all began when British field marshal Montgomery decided on an imaginative airborne operation to take Arnhem, an area north of the Rhine and deep behind the enemy lines. The Allies could then secure an important Rhine bridge that would allow Montgomery's armored forces to push up ahead from the south and stab on into Germany's industrial Ruhr and on to Berlin. "Market Garden," the code name for the largest airborne operation ever attempted, is still unknown to most people.

Relying on his own judgment and hoping that the German units north of the Rhine were disorganized and in disarray, Montgomery planned his operation with total disregard of British intelligence findings that informed him that air reconnaissance had observed two SS armored divisions with Tiger tanks within the proposed drop zone. Allied intelligence had lost track of them after Normandy and had wondered where they were. That the Germans had sent them to that specific area at that particular time for rest and relaxation was a deadly coincidence.

Around the same time as Montgomery was planning the drop, Prince Bernhard flew to liberated Belgium to inspect the Princess Irene Brigade, the Netherlands contingent of Montgomery's army. While paying the field marshal a courtesy visit in his headquarters, the Prince learned of the airborne operation. Immediately he informed the British leader that word had come from the Dutch resistance movement that units of German panzer divisions were in the area. However, the field marshal deliberately chose to ignore this report also and sent the men into battle seemingly without any concern for their lives. Committing the First Allied Airborne Army under the command of American General Louis Brereton to battle, 20,000 British, American, and Polish troops parachuted down on the peaceful heather and woods surrounding the Arnhem area. They landed right on top of the German guns. Forty-five hundred planes, including giant gliders filled with soldiers, vehicles, and supplies, participated in the operation.

Had Montgomery heeded the warnings, thousands of men would not have been riddled with bullets while helplessly floating down still strapped in their chutes. One civilian eyewitness said that the anguished cries of the young men as they were picked off in the sky was almost as loud as the sound of the murderous gunfire.

The ensuing battle lasted until September 24th, after which the remaining paratroopers either had to surrender or withdraw across the Rhine River, because a link-up with the Allied troops who had not as yet reached the south side of the bridge was impossible. It was vital for the Allies to keep the bridge intact, but the Germans had already wired it with explosives and kept up a steady barrage of machine gun fire to prevent anyone from removing them. They never succeeded in destroying it, however, for a 22-year-old Dutch student from the University of Nijmegen, Jan van Hoof, managed to run onto the bridge and disarm the charges attached to the roadway and supports.

Each year Arnhem shows a documentary called *Theirs Is the Glory* to commemorate the battle, and a few surviving paratroopers, wearing their famous red berets, return to the city. The elderly civilians who pass them on the sidewalk always smile and tip their hats in appreciation and admiration. Tears flow freely on those days.

Pieter de Vos returned to Groningen a day after the Arnhem battle and walked into our house carrying a large bulging suitcase which he opened in the hallway as soon as he saw Fietje. Spilling out were dozens of pairs of women's underwear and a man's brown suit. Stuffing an armful of the dainties into Fietje's outstretched arms, he pointed to the brown suit and said, smiling, "This is for me. I am going to leave the SS." Turning to my father who had just walked into the hallway, he said soberly, "Can you hide me for a while?" Without waiting for a reply, he walked ahead into the large bedroom, began changing, and the man who emerged minutes later looked like a well-dressed executive.

Pieter and Dad settled in the living room to discuss his fate, and with a teenager's natural curiosity, I decided to take a look at Pieter's Luger pistol while he was out of the room since I had never seen one close up before. Opening the brown holster still attached to his uniform belt which he had already stuffed in the suitcase along with his discarded uniform, I grabbed the heavy pistol, and tiptoeing softly, took it into my hiding place and later transferred it to my bedroom and under my pillow. At least now I would have something with which to protect my father should it ever become necessary!

An hour later, we had hidden the SS deserter securely in a small room dad had hurriedly constructed six feet above ground level between our house and the granary to accommodate more fugitives. Someone would pick up the suitcase containing the uniform. Dad would see to that. Before climbing into his makeshift hideout, Pieter told us of seeing hundreds of casualties on both sides. While fighting at the city, he and a few other soldiers had plundered a clothing store before deserting. "I decided to leave the SS as soon as I had shot my first paratrooper," he told us. Even though he had killed an Allied soldier, my dad decided to protect him anyway, because he seemed truly remorseful over what he'd done. Also, taking him out of circulation would mean one less soldier fighting for the German Reich.

The next day, Tuesday, September 26, 1944, was my 16th birthday, and Dad surprised me with a new suit, the first one with long pants that I had ever had. In those days most teenage boys wore either shorts or knickers, and to have a pair of long pants was a definite sign of maturity. Even though it was quite early in the morning, I had already dressed and was ready to show the world my new look. As I ate breakfast, the doorbell clanged and I heard a German voice asking my father where I was. "He is not here," Dad replied loudly, hoping I would hear him from the back room.

"I am here to induct him into the Hitler *Jugend!* Where is he?" The Germans considered anyone born of a German parent outside the border of their country as one of their own, a *Volksdeutscher* (people German) to differentiate them from those born on German soil who were called *Reichsdeutschers* (state Germans). According to their reasoning, Germany could also claim the children of a *Volksdeutscher*, which I was because of my grandfather. They felt they had the right to force me to join the Hitler *Jugend* where I would be indoctrinated as a Nazi and fight for the Fatherland if and when necessary. The occupation authorities had already written us several times, demanding that I report to their Hitler *Jugend* school. However, we had ignored each one of their reminders. My sister who was 21 years old was considered too old to be molded into a true Nazi, and the authorities never bothered her.

It only took a moment for me to scramble out the dining room window into the courtyard. Climbing hand over hand, I pulled myself up a cast iron drain pipe to a foot-wide gutter attached to the roof. I had just crawled into the gutter when from below came shouts of "Get down from there!" As I silently made a vow not to get caught, the sudden howl of air-raid sirens deafened me. If the German fighter planes really decided to intercept the American B-24s over Groningen, my life would be in real danger since the rooftop offered little protection. I cannot remember ever being more frightened than at that moment. My only thought was to get off that roof in a hurry.

Walking between where the inverted V-shaped roof of our house met that of the granary next door, I reached the front gutter of our house so that I could not be seen from the courtyard. Shifting my vision from the threat in the sky to the street below, I noticed several pedestrians pointing at me, watching my progress. Leaning against the steep slope of the roof, I inched slowly along the gutter connecting the houses until I reached the end building. Now I was trapped with nowhere to go. God had protected me thus far, I thought, but I still needed His help to get safely off the roof. I uttered a quick prayer. In my panic, I had overlooked the only possible escape route, a weathered glass cover to a ventilation shaft. Wherever it led, at least it was off the roof.

Gripping the edge of the cover with my fingers, I pulled up the lid and crawled into the shaft. Once inside with nothing to hold onto, I began to slide down feet first. Swinging wildly in the dark with my hands, I tried to find something to grab hold of and break my fall, but nothing slowed my momentum until I landed on a table in someone's kitchen and overturned a large tureen of pea soup all over my new suit. I don't remember who was more shocked at what had just occurred, me or those seated around the table ready for their midday meal. All I knew was that I was devastated as I watched the greasy stains slowly spread into the gray fabric of a suit for which I had waited five long years. The fact that I had risked my life on the roof running away from the Germans didn't seem half as bad as ruining my long-awaited birthday present.

I recall hearing a woman's shriek, but just then Dad entered the kitchen, quickly apologized for what had happened, and said, "Let's go home, Rene. They've gone now." Not anxious to climb on the roof and expose themselves to personal danger, the troopers had given up the chase and left. Once outside, the few pedestrians who had witnessed the escape clapped happily as Dad and I walked back to our house.

It was the only time the authorities tried to induct me into the Hitler *Jugend.* Apparently, they felt I wasn't worth the effort and never returned.

CHAPTER SEVEN

The Hunger-Winter

The railway strike the Dutch government-in-exile had ordered during the battle of Arnhem was both ineffective and costly for the entire country. Not only did the Germans transfer in four thousand of their own engineers and support personnel from across the border to operate the system, but they also executed several hundred of the striking railroad workers and transported others to concentration camps. General Christiansen, the German military commander for the Netherlands, and Arthur Seyss-Inquart, Hitler's personal representative, decided on still more punitive action. They would punish the country's entire population by either halting the daily shipments of potatoes, vegetables, and grain from the northern agricultural provinces of Groningen and Friesland to the western part of the country or by rerouting them to Germany. Mass starvation resulted. Coal shipments from the south, needed for heating and electric power, had already stopped because the fighting in neighboring Belgium had spilled over into Holland's southern coal mining province of Limburg.

Because of the shortages of heat, electric power, and food, the Dutch population in the west and south faced planned annihilation. The ration cards allowed for only a meager diet of 500 calories of food per day instead of the needed 2,400, if food was available at all. We did not feel much of the food shortages in Groningen both because it was located in the agricultural half of the country and because my father managed to buy all the wheat products we needed on the black market. Bread had already risen in price to 15 guilders a loaf (a day's wage for a blue-collar worker). Half a pound of margarine was now 40 guilders—almost the same price as we paid for two pounds of sugar. Groningen had the largest sugar refinery in western Europe, and during the harvest months of October and November the farmers would transport their sugar beets by truck or horsedrawn wagon to the refinery. I remember trailing behind the overloaded vehicles on my bike and picking up the sugar beets that would roll off onto the street. Stuffing as many as would fit in the saddlebags on the rear of my bike, I'd take them to my father who would slice and boil them for several hours until they had extracted all of the sugar. After removing the beet chunks, he kept the water boiling until a thick, sweet syrup remained. For a short time it was a welcome supplement to our meager sugar ration.

For a while our family did not feel the shortage of protein as others did, but after we had slaughtered the last of our goats, we then resorted to eating cow udders bought at the local slaughterhouse. After boiling the blubbery, pale white chunks for a few hours and pouring off the milky-white water, they became a good source of protein. When fried or pickled, the soft spongy meat almost tasted good—if one could forget what we were actually ingesting. As a family we were accustomed to always having meat with our meals because we erroneously believed that it was necessary for an adequate supply of protein. When the cow udders weren't available, my dad soon found another equally repulsive source of protein. The slaughterhouse had begun selling blood plasma by the liter. Now, even after so many years, I think back on those diet supplements with revulsion, but at the time our objective was to survive in any way we could.

Suspiciously eyeing a bottle of thick transparent liquid tucked under my father's arm when he came home one afternoon, I remember asking him what it was as he set it down on the kitchen table. *It looks "vies"!* (dirty, unappetizing), I remember thinking.

"Blood plasma to make an omelet," he answered apologetically. Pouring half a cup of the watery, translucent liquid into a heated frying pan covered with a thin layer of linseed oil produced something that looked like a large white omelet without the yolk. Dad was the only one in our family who tried to eat it without shuddering and having to suppress the continuous urge to vomit. But at least the cow udders and plasma were better sources of nourishment than the tulip bulbs that the starving population in the western provinces were consuming.

Word quickly filtered to members of other Adventist churches in the west that my father was always ready to assist anyone needing food. Our house soon became the destination for great numbers who walked the 75 miles or more, pushing carts or wheelbarrows with wooden wheels to buy some black market food to take back to their starving families. To accommo-date the desperate travelers, we emptied the 20 x 20 dining room of all furniture and covered the entire floor with straw mattresses. Often several members of one family would start walking to Groningen together and would be forced to leave the weakest one dead along the roadside. I remember seeing a boy, not much older than I, and his malnourished sisters crying and stumbling through a foot of snow while pushing a heavy wheelbar-row on which lay their dead father. My parents wanted to help every-one they saw but of course were unable because there just weren't enough black market provisions to go around.

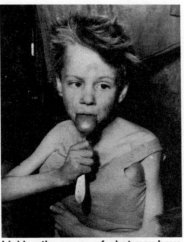

Licking the spoon of what may have been his last meal, this Dutch youngster suffered like thousands of others during the brutal "hunger-winter" of 1944-1945.

Ill-clad, starving, suffering from exposure to freezing tempera-tures, and plodding through an accumulation of two weeks of contin-uous snowfall, thousands left their homes to walk to the provinces of Groningen and Friesland. Crossing the long span of the Ijessel River bridge or the 20-mile-long dike separating the North Sea from the

A typical scene during the winter of 1944-1945. A family from one of the large cities in the west of the country walking 75 miles or more in search of food. Quite often a family member would die from starvation or exhaustion. Instead of leaving their dead father beside the road, the children of this family are taking him along in their search for food.

Yselmeer (formerly known as Zuiderzee), they sought whatever food was available. For many, death came as a welcomed release, and their bodies were sadly left behind on the frozen ground by the side of the road. Despite the overwhelming hardships to obtain food, even when they succeeded, they still faced the possibility that the Nazis would confiscate all of it at one of the roadblocks on their return trip. Barefooted children of 10 and less roamed from farm to farm in the west, pushing or pulling old baby carriages or carts in search of food.

Newborn babies left in the care of older brothers and sisters weakened and died in their cradles while their young mothers walked for miles to search for some nourishment for them. Parents praying for the death of their children so they would be beyond suffering was an everyday occurrence. Thousands died of hunger and cold during that critical winter of 1944. Large churches in Amsterdam and Rotterdam no longer were havens for the living to seek solace and reassurance. Instead those who came now were beyond any suffering and despair, for their problems were over. The living laid them out in rows on the stone floors, old next to young, until they had filled all the space. Caskets were unavailable due to the shortage of wood, and so was morgue space. The stench of the decaying bodies in the makeshift church morgues was nearly overpowering.

Because so many Dutch were dying, the Netherlands government-in-exile literally begged General Eisenhower to speed up the liberation, because, as the Dutch prime minister-in-exile pointed out in an urgent memo to the Supreme Allied Commander, "The Netherlands' government cannot accept the liberation of corpses." The country had suffered enough.

Needing to transport their troops along the shifting battle lines, the German army decided on a desperate move: to confiscate all the bicycles in the country. They started by herding hundreds of bicyclists in each city together, then trucked away their only means of transportation—their bikes. Rumors of the bicycle *razzias* spread rapidly, and those lucky enough not to get caught at that time no longer dared to venture out with their bikes but stayed home or walked. Furthermore, while the plundered country was already dying and cold, the occupation authorities now ordered us to donate one blanket per family and all high leather boots for the German troops involved in Hitler's last military gamble, the "Battle of the Bulge." It was his final major attempt to stop the American advance "toward the Fatherland."

On December 16, 1944, the German High Command committed 39 heavily armed divisions along a 50-mile front in the Ardennes Forest. Because of the element of surprise, the Germans had the initial advantage, but the Allies soon recovered their lost ground and halted the enemy offensive. Thousands perished on both sides, with Germany's casualties numbering 110,000. But like so many other battlefields, the bloody "Battle of the Bulge"—so named because of the shape of the battle line on the map—had its human interest stories as well as its tragedies.

One story I checked on about 15 years after the end of the war began on a rainy day in November 1944, a time when we were desperately holding on to life in Holland, and Hitler was still planning his Ardennes gamble. The American 28th Division had already waged a bloody and heroic battle against an experienced enemy. Knowing that his troops could not hold out much longer, General Norman D. Cota, the American Field Commander, decided to reward his men with a few weeks R&R (Rest and Relaxation), and 60 battle-worn soldiers straggled into the small picturesque Luxembourg village of Eschweiler.

"It was almost dark when they got here," Mike Huberty, one of its citizens, told me. "I still remember clearly what they looked like when they arrived. They were simply frightening! Their uniforms had been shot to pieces and were torn. Powder burns had blackened their faces, and mud covered them from head to toe. No smiles cracked their granite-like faces. The men rattled into the middle of town in their jeeps and armored cars. Although they were young, the expressions on their faces gave us the impression that they had already passed through all of the horrors of Hades. Despite the fact that they were our friends, their appearance still frightened us. We could see they needed help, so we took them in."

A family named Pletchet housed a young infantryman, George Mergenthaler. Mergenthaler soon received a reputation for his friendly attitude and helpfulness. The son of a New York millionaire, the grandson of the inventor of the linotype machine, and educated at one of America's best universities, he was a giant of a guy, but soft as a lamb. His fellow-soldiers laughed at him when he sat up several nights with one of the sick children in town, but everybody loved him. He attended church with the Eschweilers three times per week and shared his army rations with the poor. "He loved us and we loved him," one of the villagers confided to me. "He truly became one of us, and our love for each other grew."

And then came the frigid morning of December 16. The sun had barely touched the treetops when the fearful announcement, "The Germans are on the attack again," came in over the field radio. "They will be here any minute! They are headed for Eschweiler." The villagers spilled out of their houses, confused and concerned, and when "Merg" appeared outside, he was already armed, ready for action. "We didn't know what to say," Mike recalled. "Here was one of 'our' boys going to war. He beckoned us to stand around him. His face was serious and his eyes were filled with dread. He took one last look at each one of us. 'We have to fight again,' he said in a choking voice filled with tears. 'We will survive, but I am worried about you! I have to defend my home now. I hear that it won't be easy, but I will defend you till the end.'

"He gazed for the last time at each one of us. We had a feeling as though we were standing face to face with a higher power who promised us peace and rest. I don't know how to explain it, but suddenly our fear was gone," Mike related. "Putting his arm around the shoulder of Father Dodsen, the elderly Catholic priest of the village church, George sighed wearily, 'Don't be afraid, Pastor, for I will defend you.'"

After those words George climbed into the back seat of the waiting jeep, right behind the heavy machine gun, and left town in the direction of the thundering gunfire.

When the battle ended and no word came from Mergenthaler, everyone in the small town began to search for him in the forest nearby. The Americans had won the battle, but their beloved friend was missing. Everyone in town knew that if he were able, nothing would keep George from returning to Eschweiler. The Pletchet sisters were searching the outskirts of their town for battlefield graves when suddenly they noticed at the edge of a narrow snow-covered forest path two flat stones on the ground over which a hurriedly made cross of two small branches had fallen. Overturning the stones, they stared into Merg's frozen face. He was still wearing the blue sweater they had knitted for him a week before the battle.

All of Eschweiler cried when they reburied him in the small village cemetery. Even though his family eventually claimed his body and reinterred him in their family tomb in the United States, Eschweiler did not forget their adopted American son. They dedicated the town's church to him. The Great Seal of the United States in the stained glass window in the left wall of the sanctuary and the stained glass window showing Saint George killing the dragon on the right constantly remind the townspeople of "their" George who gave his life for Eschweiler. But even more impressive than those windows is the giant mural on the wall behind the altar of the simple Catholic church. It pictures George Mergenthaler, life-size, with his battle fatigues clearly showing under an open blue robe. Kneeling before Christ as one of His pupils, he hands out bread to the poor.

And while the bloody war for Europe's freedom raged on, and our liberation came closer, the Dutch were still dying from hunger. To minimize the chances of an open revolt, the local authorities in several of the major cities sought and received permission from their German overseers to set up "Central Kitchens" where they made meager meals available on an irregular basis. The central kitchen in the city of Schiedam near Rotterdam served boiled porridge made from cattle fodder.

At the same time, German troops transported in secret to the major cities, began rounding up all men between 17 and 40 years of age. Tens of thousands taken in the mass-*razzias* found themselves trucked to areas where the Germans wanted more fortifications dug. More than 20,000 emaciated men were forced from their families and marched off, while another 20,000 vanished in cattle wagons in easterly (German) directions. About the same number of men descended into the lice and flea-infested holds of empty Rhine cargo vessels. The Germans would drop them off across the Zuiderzee. Some of those who survived the forced labor said that the men had so many fleas and lice on them that their ragged clothes were more alive than those who wore them.

For fuel to warm those left at home, the people demolished the apartments and houses that had formerly belonged to the deported Jews and removed all the wood along with the wooden ties from many of the streetcar tracks. The schools had long ago closed.

One day during that desperate season, my dad felt suddenly impressed to load his bicycle with bread, oil, wheat, and meat stuffed into two sets of canvas saddlebags, one mounted on the luggage carrier, the other on the handlebars.

"Where are you going with that food?" I remember asking him.

"To the Eelsings in Utrecht," he said quietly, obviously not looking forward to plowing over a hundred miles through the snow. Hendrik Eelsing was his closest friend and a church administrator who lived in Utrecht. "He needs me. I know it!"

Pushing instead of pedaling his bike over the icy snow-packed roads, he fought his way through the still falling snow, his prayers coming just as fast as his asthmatic breathing.

"I almost lost everything at the Rhine River roadblock," he related to us after his return 10 days later. Several times, his limbs half frozen and nearly blinded by the falling snow, he had crawled on his knees, dragging the loaded bike behind him. When he finally reached the outskirts of Utrecht, he pulled the heavily loaded bike to the front of his friend's house and collapsed noisily against the door, not having the strength left to knock.

Hendrik and Heike, his wife, had been on their knees, praying for food. Their teenage children, Annie and Wim, were in bed asleep, trying to escape the relentless pangs of hunger that always tormented them when they were awake. Hearing a sound at the front door, Hendrik stood up and blurted out, "That's Noordje with food, Heike! God sent him just in time. Now we can eat again." Running out of the living room and down the narrow steps to the front door, he caught my dad, who, leaning against the door, was still sliding down to the ice-covered pavement. "Noordje, God sent you! We were just praying for food!" The tears flowed freely down the cheeks of both men.

At another crucial point during that "hunger-winter," Pastor Eelsing asked my father to help feed the children in an Adventist-sponsored youth home near Utrecht. Using his own money, Dad managed to buy large quantities of bread, wheat, butter, meat, oil, and potatoes on the black market. Generously bribing the sergeant of the German motor pool around the corner, he obtained the services of a five-ton truck and uniformed driver and headed for Zonheuvel, the children's home. With his German driver, a counterfeit *Ausweis* identifying him as a provincial Nazi food commissioner, and a Nazi swastika pin on his lapel, he managed to bluff his way through every

German checkpoint and successfully delivered his truckload of provisions to the needy children.

One night, soon after his return, a pounding at the front door startled us, after which three Gestapo agents, four of the S.D. (security service), and two uniformed Feldgendarmerie (military police) soldiers stomped into the hallway. When we saw them brandishing their Mauser machine pistols in the crooks of their arms, we knew that word must have leaked out that we were hiding an SS deserter. Why else the Feldgendarmerie? They never took part in ordinary *razzias*. My heart thumped loudly in my chest, even more than when I heard the Allied bombers flying overhead on their nighttime runs to Germany. I was sure everyone in the room was having the same reaction. The S.D.s were frightening enough, but to see them accompanied by the Gestapo and the feared Feldgendarmerie, I knew this was to be the worst *Razzia* yet.

The two tough-looking military policemen wore on their uniforms the unique marks of their authority, large shoulder-to-shoulder silver breastplates in the shape of a crescent moon embossed with the words, "Feldgendarmerie." The shields hung on heavy silver chains around their necks, and with each step clinked against the metal buttons on their uniforms. Pointing their machine pistols in our direction, they motioned for us to line up against the wall and snarled, "*Hände hoch!* (hands high)."

The Germans had certainly picked the most inopportune night for a raid, for in the room were my parents, my sister, her friend Fietje, and three fugitives: Flip, the young Jew who had been in hiding since the moment he had received orders to report for transportation to a concentration camp in 1941; Jack van der Mei, a friend of our family and half Jewish; and Pieter, the SS soldier who had deserted after the Battle of Arnhem. Holding us at gunpoint, the Germans demanded, "*Ihre Ausweise, bitte!* (Your identification cards, please)."

I still remember Pieter standing erect between Jack and Flip, as though he was at attention. *That sure is a dead give-away,* I thought to myself. *They'll know for sure he's a former soldier.* But at that moment the raiding party was more interested in Flip and Jack than us, trying to find out who they really were and what they were doing at our home that late at night after curfew. Most of the loud questioning seemed to go right over my head, but the accusation *"Ihr seid Juden* (you are Jews)" shouted in the faces of Jack and Flip clearly registered in my mind that night. I also remember the Feldgendarmerie giving Pieter a thorough interrogation, but luckily all of our guests had the best of counterfeit ID cards, complete with "official" German swastika stamps.

The waves of panic we were all experiencing during the interrogation, so obvious to our intruders, seemed to increase their desire to intimidate us even more. They really enjoyed what they were doing. I couldn't stop shaking for at least 15 minutes during the flurry of questioning as the Gestapo agents considered who to take with them and what to do with our visitors. They finally decided to return everyone's ID cards except my father's and mine. Gruffly telling us to report to Gestapo headquarters for more interrogation the next morning, they quickly left. The memory of the flickering candlelight reflecting in the silver breastplates of the departing Feldgendarmerie as they backed out of the room lingered with me for many years. The thought of being ordered to Scholtenshuis, the "torture-house-of-no-return," absolutely terrified me.

"Why take just our ID cards? We are the least important here," Dad kept saying over and over. I remember thinking that perhaps the Gestapo wanted to interrogate him about the underground, using me as leverage, but somehow I didn't dare to divulge my suspicions to anyone. Leaving us alone with our problems, our fugitive guests quickly slipped back to their hiding places, Jack and Flip to the granary and Pieter to crawl into the narrow attic between the house and the granary.

"Noorbergen, what did you do to deserve all that high-powered attention last night? The entire block was sealed off with German soldiers!" one of our neighbors asked my father the next morning. By 10:00 o'clock that day we were standing in front of Gestapo headquarters. One of the sentries ushered us into the building. *"Zweite Stock!* (second floor)," he said, pointing to the staircase ahead of us. Tremblingly, we climbed the brown wooden steps, holding firmly onto each other's hand.

"What will they do to us?" I still remembered hearing the screams of the tortured when I had passed the building some time before. "Will that happen to us? Will they torture us too?"

A guard seated at a desk in the hallway at the top of the stairs asked our names, checked a list, and pointed toward a door further down the hall. *"Sie müssen da sein!* (That's where you have to be)," he hissed. We knocked, softly at first, then harder when we received no response. For 15 minutes nothing happened, then the clicking of high heels that had started at the far end of the hallway, stopped behind us.

"Was müssen Sie hier?" a sweet voice interrupted our mounting terror.

"We were told to report here to be questioned and get our ID cards back," my father answered. A minute later the young woman in her German army uniform slipped in front of us, reached for the doorknob, and entered the office.

"Warten Sie ein Moment, bitte (Wait a moment, please)," she suggested, turning her head toward us as she hurried in. Wasting little time, she quickly opened a drawer and returned with our ID cards. Shoving them into our eager hands, she whispered loudly, *"Macht schnell!* (Get out of here quickly). *Macht schnell,"* she repeated again with great urgency while she gestured to the desk guard to let us pass. He then gave the same signal to the man stationed inside the front door, and we left, not quite believing as yet that the young uniformed woman had miraculously opened the gate of "terror house" for us.

Nobody had asked any questions. We could finally breathe freely again for the first time since we had entered the building 30 minutes earlier. *Could she have been the angel we had prayed for while climbing the stairs?* I thought. *What a miracle! No interrogation or Gestapo.*

It was not until after the war that we heard of others who also had been helped by a German girl in Gestapo headquarters. Could she perhaps have been the one who had intervened and saved our lives? I know that had it not been for his guardian angel, my father's life would have ended long before his 83rd year, 38 years after the war. As we left

I clutched my ID card so tightly in my coat pocket that when I finally took it out of my pocket, it looked like a gigantic spitball from the pressure of my sweaty hand.

"Do I believe in guardian angels?" Of course I do, for I have experienced too many narrow escapes during the war and in my work as a foreign and war correspondent over the years since then, not to believe in them. I have only to let my mind drift back to being captured and released by Moslem rebels in Beirut in 1958, to being with a lost jungle patrol in Laos, meeting head on with a Chinese infantry squad on night patrol in Korea's no-man's-land, making an emergency landing with a National Guard artillery plane on fire over the Bakersfield mountains in central California, as well as my current cardiovascular problems.

When my father and I talked afterward about our miraculous escape, he related to me something that had happened when he was still a small boy. One evening after staying too long at a friend's house, he had to walk home alone in the dark. Thoroughly frightened by imaginary monsters behind every tree and around every corner, he flung open the door of his house and ran inside. As he glanced fearfully down the dimly lit hallway, he noticed someone scurry into his room carrying a candle-lit lantern. Unable to grasp the significance of what he had just seen, he jumped into bed and under the covers. During the night he awoke from a troubled sleep and saw a bright shining being sitting on the chair beside his bed. Instinctively he knew it was his guardian angel. "Don't be frightened, Rinke," the being said soothingly. "You are safe, nothing will happen to you. Just go back to sleep. I will stay here and protect you."

The continuing hunger in occupied Holland drove many to desperation. A unit of the resistance movement, needing a German staff car for a planned operation, ambushed a German BMW convertible staff car on a main highway near Apeldoorn on March 7, 1945. While checking the wreckage the following morning the police discovered that it contained the body of the "Hohere SS und SD Polizei Fuhrer" Rauter (the highest SS and SD commander). In reprisal, his second in command executed 117 already imprisoned members of the resistance movement.

By April 1945 the hunger in the country had reached catastrophic proportions. Tens of thousands had already starved to death and still more were slated to become part of the hundreds of thousands of innocent civilians that would succumb by war's end.

Negotiations between the Allied powers and Seyss-Inquart, the German commissioner for the Netherlands, finally resulted in a dramatic life-saving gesture by the American and British air forces. Eisenhower ordered that they drop food in giant parcels and contain-

SS chief Rauter, who was ambushed by the Dutch resistance while riding in his staff car. The Germans executed hundreds of Dutch in retaliation.

ers over the densely populated cities of Western Holland. Preparations for the mission began on the airfields of the U.S. and British air forces in England around the middle of April. For five long days and nights, all available personnel stowed cement bags filled with powdered potatoes, dried vegetables, dried meat, margarine, sugar, and dried eggs into the bomb bays of hundreds of squadrons of Lancaster and B-24 bombers. Many of the pilots who had previously sown nothing but death and destruction on their bombing missions, cried openly when on Sunday, April 29, they received the command to take off.

Once they reached the Dutch coast, the planes flew so low that they almost touched the red-tiled rooftops where some people were already standing and waving flags and sheets in anticipation of finally getting something to eat. Radio Vrij Nederland, broadcasting from London, had already announced that food was on the way. It was like manna from heaven, and amazingly, the German fighter planes did

Rauter's ambushed staff car.

not interfere. This time Seyss-Inquart kept his word. He knew that one violation of the accord to allow the Allies to save the Dutch population would certainly make him the target of a lynch mob. The mission did not stop with one wave of planes, but lasted five days during which time the planes dropped 5,000 tons of food supplies on open fields, streets, and rooftops.

Prince Bernhard commented afterwards, "My entire staff and I lived during the last weeks before the capitulation around the end of April under tremendous tension, because saving as many Netherlanders as possible from starvation had become the most important issue to us."

The "bombings" of cities with food did not include the provinces of Groningen or Friesland in the north with their capital cities of Groningen and Leeuwarden because they had managed to survive on their own hoarded and black market supplies. Nevertheless the people there shared in the happiness the food drops brought to the rest of the country.

Aside from the food supplies, what sustained us more than anything else was the hope of our soon *bevrijding* (liberation). Freedom was in the air—we could smell it! Even we youngsters talked about nothing else. It was something we all looked forward to. Henny Smit, my friend across the street who had been confined to his bed with tuberculosis and had been lying in front of a bay window overlooking the street for more than a year, also talked of nothing else

Loading food supplies in a B-24 bomber at a British airfield. The food would go to the starving cities of western Holland.

Allied bombers dropping food over occupied Holland.

but the long-awaited liberation.

"On my first day out of bed, I want to take a long walk down the street with the two of you," he whispered longingly, but weakly, to me and another friend whenever we visited him. Little did we know that shortly thereafter the three of us would take that long walk down the street, but Henny would not know it.

CHAPTER EIGHT

From Nightmare to Awakening

Our family had not as yet recovered from Uncle Gijs' capture by the Gestapo a few weeks earlier when rumors of a soon liberation began circulating wildly. "The Canadian army is on the way," people told each other in the streets. "The Germans are in full retreat!" Feeding the rumors was the sight of German camouflaged army trucks roaring in and out of the gate of the garrison barracks around the corner. The flocks of thousands of B-24s and Lancaster bombers that flew overhead on their daily bombing runs to the German port cities also did much to increase the optimism we all felt.

It was on Friday, April 13, 1945, when it all began to burst loose in Groningen. In the meantime, the rumor-mill had already brought news that a separate war had erupted on Texel, one of the picturesque islands off the northern coast of Holland and situated between the North Sea and the Waddenzee. Located amidst the coastal sand flats, where small dead trees anchored in blocks of concrete served to indicate the deep-water channels to the coastal harbors, it was one of the vacation islands where I had spent much of my youth.

I recall my father coming home one day and blurting out, "Do you remember the lighthouse on Texel and the lighthouse keeper's home at its foot. Can you believe that his house and the buildings around it have been destroyed in a battle between the Russians and the Germans?"

"How did the Russians get there?" I asked in astonishment. "The

Russians are fighting the Germans on the eastern front in Russia, aren't they? How did they get to Texel?"

"These were prisoners of war whom the German army transported there to keep out of their way. That's all I've heard," he answered, equally puzzled by the news. It was not until the early 1950s, while in Holland on a vacation from the United States, that I had a chance to investigate what really had transpired during that time.

Sadly I stood at the edge of a small cemetery amidst stately fir trees and slowly advancing wild shrubbery, trying to piece together what should be considered one of the most courageous episodes of World War II. With his name on an ornate and artistically designed grave marker, the Russian officer, Captain Loladse Schalwa, lies at the head of the remains of his 476 men: With them he unleashed a revolt against the powerful German army. They were the victors and the losers at the same time and are destined to remain there forever in the sandy soil of this peaceful island because of a deliberate lack of Allied help.

Loladse Schalwa, leader of the revolt against the Germans on the island of Texel.

Jac Keijzer, former commander of the Dutch Interior Forces (the resistance movement) on the island, and coconspirator of Captain Loladse, shared the sad story with me of the unsuccessful revolt as we leisurely walked among the ruins of an old farm and between the concrete bunkers not far from the foot of the lighthouse.

"This was the spot of the final battle," Jac whispered softly. The relentless roar of the stormy surf pounding the coastline of the island and the piercing screams of hundreds of circling sea gulls added a measure of pathos to his sad recollections. "It's been several years ago," he continued, "but incidents of the rebellion have lodged themselves so deeply within my memory that it seems as if it happened only a few days ago."

"Jac, how did the Russians get here?" I asked, absentmindedly kicking some of the seashells that were lying on the sandy path ahead of me.

"They started out as German prisoners of war," he answered, "but decided to enlist in the German army to escape the horrors of being tortured and systematically starved to death in a Russian POW camp in Germany. Stalin once remarked," Jac Keijzer said, "that a soldier can still fight for his country as a prisoner, so they decided to enlist in the German army and sabotage it from within."

There were 800 of them, and together with 400 Germans they formed the Georgian infantry battalion.

"These Russians, who arrived here on January 10, 1945, were the second group of Russians who had come to the island," Keijzer explained. "The first were a battalion of Caucasian infantry, and we as resistance leaders had agreed with their officers to an armed revolt against the German garrison on the island. The German High Command in Holland probably became suspicious of the friendly relations that developed between us, and suddenly they were transferred away from here. In their place came the Georgians. They had been here but a short time when one of their officers came to my house and said, 'We want to work with you on the same basis as you agreed to with the Caucasians.' "

Keijzer decided to relay their request to headquarters in England for the final decision.

Before parting that evening, the two men agreed to become better acquainted first and establish a mutual trust before finalizing the plans for the rebellion. No one knows how the German military commander for the Netherlands became suspicious of the friendship between the islanders and the new arrivals, but soon he summoned the commander of the mixed battalion to his headquarters on the mainland for consultation. It was at that point that Artemidse, the political commissar of the Russian contingent, began to sense danger and decided to act. "He came to me on March 31," Keijzer continued, "and said that the time for action had arrived. If you can get me a doctor who can give me a contagious disease, then I will have a reason to see our battalion Red Cross and will probably be sent to a hospital on the mainland. From there I will be able to contact our party members in Amsterdam."

Keijzer was not able to get a doctor to grant Artemidse's request, so the Russians decided not to wait any longer with their plans for a revolt. During the early morning hours of April 6, they slaughtered most of the German garrison on the island. More than 400 Germans lost their lives during that first day. The rebellion continued until the afternoon of April 20, when the Canadian troops under General Crerar had already completed Groningen's liberation.

"When the first day of the revolt was over, Artemidse admitted to me that he was personally responsible for at least 20 German deaths. When one of his men refused to kill a sleeping German soldier, he asked, 'Why?' and the soldier responded, 'I have to wake him up first so that he can make his peace with God.' " Turning to me, Keijzer exclaimed, "Isn't that a strange reaction from a communist soldier?" I had to agree.

The fighting continued with the cooperation of members of the resistance movement on the island. At one point during the revolt, the Russian Captain Loladse gathered together his men and the Dutch fighters at Texla, the bunker complex near De Burg, the sleepy island's main village, and hoisted the Dutch tri-color flag. Raising his arm, he yelled proudly and triumphantly, "Long live Soviet Russia and long live Holland." At the time he did not know that in den Helder, the nearest city on the mainland, the alarm sirens were already howling. The German command on that former Dutch naval base had received an urgent message from a transmitter located in one of the German bunkers not as yet taken by the Russians. Within hours, armored units of the Herman Goering SS Division, which happened to be in the vicinity, began landing on Texel, after shelling it with heavy artillery.

Still counting on Allied help from England, Loladse and his men continued fighting against unbelievable odds. The details of their heroic stand reached us in Groningen after the SS forces had already massacred them.

"The arrival of the German troops caused a moment of confusion among Loladse and his men," Keijzer told me. "When I heard that Germans were landing on the island, I rushed over to Loladse and told him, but he just shrugged it off. Twice more I checked with my people outside, and each time the information was the same. The Germans were landing! I told Loladse again," Jac recalled, excitedly, "but his reaction was the same. He just could not believe that they were German soldiers and not the Allies coming to help. Only when the heavy German artillery began to shell the island did he reluctantly believe. As the first rounds screamed overhead, he suddenly realized in a bewildered way that Germany was not yet defeated, and he would have to fight to the death.

" 'Perhaps all is not lost as yet,' he whispered sadly, his brown eyes filling with tears of disappointment. 'I still have most of my men,' " he added, trying to bolster his courage. By now the SS had supplemented the artillery barrage with tanks and bayonet-wielding and flame-throwing infantry. Threatened by bullets, bayonets, and scorching flames, the Georgians found themselves pushed back, fighting heroically from bunker to bunker. Many of the islanders risked their own lives by providing them shelter and food until the SS began to form a living chain of soldiers, systematically combing the island from coast to coast, searching every bush, house, and bunker. The hand-to-hand combat between SS forces and Russian rebels mounted in frequency and intensity, and every Russian soldier that died did so while glancing in the direction of the stormy sea, hoping to catch a glimpse of the Allied reinforcements that they wanted to believe were on the way to help them.

The SS burned any houses and farms where escaping Russians might be hiding. The dense black smoke and the angry flames hungrily licking the sky revealed how far the living chain of SS searchers had come. The organized Dutch resistance movement began to make plans to seek help for the Russians in England by taking the large life-saving boat "Joan Hudson," a vessel permanently stationed in the island's harbor for North Sea rescues. A few crawled aboard unnoticed by the German guards and roared away through the heavy breakers.

Reaching England a day later without being intercepted or challenged by any German navy patrol boats or fighter planes, they reported the highlights of the battle to the Allied High Command. The Allied leaders decided that since the total capitulation of the entire German army might only be a matter of days away, it was too costly to help the Russians—and, for some unknown reason, too dangerous to the Allied cause!

As a result, the Russians continued to fight, but no one could find Loladse. Hiding out in a farm torched by the SS, he survived the flames and managed to crawl out of the basement when the heat became too intense. But then an SS squad intercepted and shot him without realizing that they had just killed the much wanted leader of the rebellion.

One of the Russians, Sergeant Silosanni, together with a well-armed group of rebels, broke through the German lines and began attacking the enemy from the rear, but the main battle actually centered around the old lighthouse. When most of the Russians had run out of ammunition, they surrendered. In revenge, the Germans compelled the Russian prisoners to dig their own graves, after which they executed them in a most savage way and kicked the bodies into the holes. Their agonizing death cries could be heard across the dunes, and the islanders wept.

Even the civilian population of the island suffered severe casualties. One hundred and seventeen were shot or burned in the battle, and more than 30 lost their lives in front of SS firing squads. When the entire German army finally surrendered on May 7, 1945, the island of Texel still remained in German hands, and fighting between the surviving Russian soldiers and the SS continued fiercely until the liberating Canadian troops arrived on May 20. The total number of people killed in that revolt was between 2,000 and 2,500 Russians, Germans, and Dutch civilians, including resistance fighters.

And while the remaining 229 Russian soldiers fought for their lives among the sand dunes of the island and in cold concrete bunkers of the Atlantic Wall, Holland was being liberated, the Russian army was taking Berlin, and Adolf Hitler committed suicide with Eva Braun, his wife of less than one day. The trip home for the Russian survivors finally began on June 17 when, as Allied soldiers with special status, the Canadians transported them to the Russian command in Germany.

Back in Russia, they were received as heros. "I once listened to a special broadcast about them from Radio Moscow," Jac said. "I clearly recognized the voice of Artemidse, and in a letter he wrote me a while back he mentioned that a reunion of the surviving Russians had taken place. Before their departure from the island, the Georgians expressed their deep thanks to the people of Texel, and said that 'in the future our history books will mention the heroic population of Texel, and the entire Soviet Union will know about the small country of Holland. We are leaving now to return home, but our friendship will be forever.'

"Since the war the Russian survivors have returned to the island several times to visit the graves of those they had to leave behind," Jac concluded. And while relations between East and West fluctuate between cold war and *glasnost,* Loladse and his men lie peacefully among the islanders they loved.

Back in Groningen, we were bracing for a fight. Rumors flew back and forth about our expected liberation, but it did not occur until shortly after 4:30 of the afternoon of April 13 when we began to hear a strange but insistent rumbling in the air, like distant thunder. "That's from the Canadian artillery," my dad said excitedly when he arrived home around supper time. "I hear that they are approaching the city with big cannons and hundreds of tanks. It is the best news we've heard in a long time, and we'd better gather some food and blankets together and head for the basement. Don't worry about the house. It has survived many other wars, and it will survive this one," he reassured my trembling mother. Usually we spent our Friday nights studying our Bible lessons seated around the dining room table with a kerosene lamp as the only illumination. This night my father was only concerned for the safety of his family. I wanted to believe that it was indeed the beginning of our liberation, but after waiting so long, I had almost begun to accept the idea that it would never happen.

Quickly everyone grabbed their *vluchtkoffertjes* (escape suitcases), packed some provisions, and fled to the basement through the courtyard entrance. With the women safely underground, Dad and I made one more dash upstairs to look out the living room windows overlooking the street. We could see no pedestrians or bicyclers. The only movement came from a few German trucks and motorcycles racing by, heading east in the direction of Germany. We then joined my trembling mother, Dina, and Fietje, who were sitting on a few crates close to two small front windows that also overlooked the street about one foot above ground level. "Would we be safe?" was the question we asked ourselves as we settled down for the night.

"Just stay out of sight," dad kept warning us whenever we got too close to the windows. Other than hearing the thunder from the artillery and seeing a reddish glow hanging over the old city center, we passed the night uneventfully.

The next morning brought no surprises either. But in the afternoon, as Allied bombers moved across the skies heading for Germany far above the lingering black smoke of the burning buildings below, I peeked curiously through one of the basement windows. Crouching against the houses on the opposite side of the canal, a single German soldier stealthily moved in the direction of the already vacated German barracks. Suddenly he turned and looked directly at me. Raising his rifle, he carefully aimed it. I realized the danger I was in but somehow couldn't pull myself away from the window. My mind said to move, but my legs wouldn't respond.

Before he could pull the trigger, however, a shot rang out, and I saw him spin sideways and crumple to the sidewalk. Blood oozed from a round hole that had appeared in his chest and his face had frozen in a shocked grimace. We had not seen any Canadian soldiers as yet, so the shot must have come from a member of the resistance who had been on our side of the street and saw the danger.

Shifting my attention to Henny Smit's house, I saw the door open and my friend standing on the threshold. It was his first day out of bed after having been bedridden for more than a year. The time we had been looking forward to had finally arrived. As I watched Henny, a German military motorcycle with a sidecar crossed the bridge at the beginning of our street. The moment he passed Henny and saw him standing in the doorway, the helmeted sidecar passenger raised his machine pistol and fired a few rounds at the unsuspecting teenager. I saw Henny twirl around, his arms outstretched, and his mouth opened in a silent scream. As he fell backward into the hallway, his father who was standing close by caught Henny's body in his arms and together they slowly sank to the floor. I knew then that we would never take that long walk down the street as we had planned to do on his first day out.

Anger, hatred, and sadness gripped me as I recoiled in horror from the window. "They've just shot Henny Smit for no reason," I stammered to my dad, turning around. "The *mof* just used my friend for target practice. He's dead. Is there nothing we can do to stop them?"

"We can help the others in liberating Groningen," he replied sadly and decidedly. "We've got to help get the Germans out of here. God cannot expect us to just sit here and let those murderers escape their punishment." My mother, ashen-faced, softly cried. The Sabbath was far from peaceful that weekend. While none had been tranquil since the Germans had overrun the country, this was the worst one yet. We had just witnessed two violent deaths mere minutes apart within a few hundred feet of our house, and hearing the continuous rumbling of the Canadian artillery, we knew that we could expect more violence and more deaths.

Even though we had been waiting for this day for five long years, the realization that the liberation would bring days of terrifying street fighting was a frightening thought. I remember my dad reading the twenty-third psalm and praying for our safety. The sound of the heavy guns continued throughout the night.

The next morning he and I carefully slid out of the house, trying to ignore the protests of my mother and sister. I knew he was concerned about my accompanying him, but I still felt that in some way my being along might be helpful. He was unarmed, as he always was, but I had taken the Luger out of its hiding place and tucked it in between my belt as an added precaution. While I didn't know if I could pull the trigger, I now had the means to protect my father should it become necessary. His life was too precious to me to take any chance of his losing it now.

The city center was still smoldering as the barrage from the 25-pounder cannons continued, hitting among other sites the anti-aircraft emplacement with its batteries of ack-ack guns adjacent to the nearby canal locks. The bombardment was preparing the way for the Sherman and Stuart tanks and the infantry of General Bruce's Second Canadian Division, part of the First Canadian Army, led by General H.D.G. Crerar.

Even though the city walls of Groningen had been torn down years before, the strategic canals surrounding the old city had remained, and 14 bridges facilitated the flow of traffic to the newer sections of the city. The Germans could have destroyed each one with well-placed explosive charges, but they neglected to do so because they ignored the possibility of a full scale Allied attack on the city. The bridge at the beginning of our street was known as the Steentil-brug (bridge #1). The next one was the Poelebrug (bridge #2).

When dad and I left the house, we turned left in the direction of the Steentilbrug and then right along the canal until we reached the Poelebrug. Stopping there, we joined a group of fellow Groningers who were as curious as we were about the progress of the battle for the city. No German was in sight, but members of the Interior Forces were busy rounding up Dutch Nazis and dragging them, screaming and cursing, out of their homes.

It was at that point that we heard heavy machine-gun fire near bridge #3, directed at a long cylindrical object with fins laying in the middle of bridge #2. Although the Canadians were ready to cross the bridge to reach our section of the city, they could not see the position of the machine gun nest. While a few members of the resistance began firing at the machine gunners, disabling at least two of them, I slipped behind my father and dashed for the other side of the bridge to alert the Canadians as to the location of the German gunners.

Allied troops during the liberation of the Netherlands.

About halfway across the gunfire resumed again. My impetuous-ness could have gotten me killed, but at the time all I could think of was reaching the other side of the bridge to warn the Canadians. With bullets pinging next to me, I dove behind the only object that could conceal me, the bomb that the Germans were trying to detonate. Laying flat on my stomach with my heart pounding loudly in my chest, I could hear the machine gun bullets ricocheting off the other side of the bomb. At the next pause in the firing, I jumped up and zigzagged to the other end of the bridge where a smiling Canadian captain with two pistols strapped on his hips greeted me with a tight hug.

After I explained why I had come, a squad of soldiers entered one of the corner row houses and climbed to the top floor. There they stepped into the wide gutter extending from house to house to the end of the block.

I was already on the other side of the canal and had rejoined my father, when we saw the Canadians drop a number of hand grenades

Canadian tanks liberating Groningen, the author's hometown.

down on the German machine gunners. The firing stopped, and the bridges remained intact. The liberation could continue unhindered.

Nearing home, we noticed a number of men pushing or hauling carts loaded with stacks of canned food across a narrow road at the end of the canal. "Food! They have food!" we both exclaimed. Within minutes we had extricated the wheelbarrow from our crowded basement and joined the line to the warehouses.

Impatient to finally get their chance to grab German Army food supplies, a number of Groningers had forced the locks and began plundering the two 3-story warehouses. Traffic to and from the storage places increased steadily as everyone wanted a share for his family. Remaining with the wheelbarrow and Dad's bike with the huge saddlebags on the rear, Fietje, who had also come along, and I waited while he went inside from floor to floor collecting needed food supplies, such as canned butter, chocolate, canned beef, beans, etc.

To assure that no marauding German patrols would interfere, two Canadian Sherman tanks had taken up positions across the canal with their cannons and heavy machine guns trained on the warehouses. That side of the canal had already been liberated, but we were still in German hands, and what we were doing was punishable by death.

After collecting as much as we could handle, we started for home across the narrow road near the old gatekeeper's house. Dad and Fietje ran ahead to drop off his load so that he could return to help me with the wheelbarrow for the last 500 feet. As I nervously stood on the street corner with my precious supplies, I suddenly heard German voices coming from my right out of sight of the Canadian tanks. There they were — grim-faced helmeted soldiers with rifles strapped on their backs — a military bicycle patrol heading my way.

If I run now, they'll see me for sure, but if I stay here, they'll shoot me, my mind raced. I knew also that my father realized my desperate situation as he watched from across the street but was totally helpless to do anything about it. Unfortunately I was on my own. Praying that they hadn't seen me standing by the wheelbarrow, I reacted in the only way I could. Dropping to the cobblestone street, I played dead.

As I lay with my head facing the curb, I could tell they were nearly upon me because their muffled conversation had become more clear and audible. When I sensed that they were almost adjacent to my inert body, I took a deep breath and held it until I thought my lungs would burst. I kept wondering if they would use me for target practice like they had done Henny. The wheels of their bikes had approached to within a few feet of my head when I heard one of them say, *"Kuk mal, der tote Käsekopf!* (Look at that dead cheesehead [the German slang for Dutchman])." Then they were past me. *They didn't kill me! They went on by!* I couldn't believe it. The feeling of relief was indescribable. Laying on my side, I could see through the slits in my eyelids the bikes disappearing out of my field of vision, and only then did I feel safe to move again. Once the patrol was out of sight, my father rushed over to me and together we pushed home our "liberated" supplies, both silently thanking our God for saving my life.

Later that day, Dad and I grew curious as to how successful the Canadians had been in routing the Germans, and headed for the city park. It was still the scene of severe house-to-house and tree-to-tree fighting, a fact we realized too late as we heard the firing of the small Stuart tanks close by. But it was the constant rifle fire that made us decide to take cover in one of the still unaffected side streets. From our vantage point, we saw Canadian infantry soldiers crawling toward the trenches in the park in which a strange mixture of German troops had taken up positions—regular Wehrmacht soldiers, elderly reserves (men in their late 50s and early 60s) as well as Groningen's Hitler *Jugend* (youths between 10 and 16), who had been forced to make a last ditch defense.

Their rifle-fire was more of an annoyance than a danger to the advancing Canadian infantry troops, but in order to minimize possible losses, the four-ton weapons carrier spit 90-foot-long streams of liquid fire from their flame-throwers into the trenches. Out came screaming khaki-uniformed members of the Hitler *Jugend,* burning like torches. It was a sight I would never forget—young human beings in short pants totally aflame, crawling and running, crying loudly, "Mommy! Oh Mommy, help me! *(help mij) Ik ga dood!* (I am dying)." The screams became louder the further they ran. Several were mercifully shot as they tried to reach safety.

While the fighting for the possession of the city continued, the resistance rounded up Dutch girls who had dated German soldiers to receive—what we considered, at least—their just punishment. Surrounded by scores of jeering people, they had their hair shaved off after which someone painted a red swastika on their shiny heads.

Sometime during those turbulent hours, our mute cabinetmaker dropped by to see how we had survived. Learning about Henny's death, he volunteered to stay and help us construct a simple casket of small boards and a sheet of hardboard, the only material we had available. Afterward we carried it across the street and placed the body of my friend inside. Then we set it on two sawhorses in his family's garage. As I noticed the droplets of blood leaking from the cracks in the casket, I could feel warm tears running down my cheeks. "Sorry, Henny," I whispered. "Goodbye. I'll miss you."

It was a time of utter confusion for the few remaining Nazis and sympathizers as well as for the German soldiers, whose only goal now was to escape death and become prisoners of war. Many, however, did not wait for the uncertain status of POW and decided to run for it, managing to get as far as the small Dutch cities of Appingedam and Delfzijl, about 40 miles from Groningen in an easterly direction.

When I rejoined the Boy Scouts in the early days after the battle for Groningen, the authorities asked us to help the Interior Forces guard the crossroads near Appingedam. It was evening when our troop set up camp alongside the railroad tracks in the meadow of a former Dutch Nazi farmer. All of us felt quite important in our role of assistant guards, but our bravado suddenly vaporized the next morning, when sticking our heads outside the pup tents, we saw little wooden stakes all around us—especially between our tents and the road—and attached to them were small flags displaying skulls and crossbones and the words, *Achtung—Minen.* We had set up camp in a German mine field!

After we all had managed to survive five harrowing years of war, it would be the height of irony to get blown apart by a land mine after it was over. Crawling carefully with our hastily dismantled tents and our camping equipment strapped to our backs, we tried to identify where our footsteps had matted the grass the previous evening and somehow managed to reach the road safely. Needless to say, we moved to a more secure field the following night.

It was my turn to stand guard that evening alongside of an adult member of the Interior Forces. We were to watch for possible enemy stragglers on their way to the border 20 miles away. The man carried a rifle, and I and the others had fastened our scout knives to the end of five-foot-long sticks to use as spears. Sometime during the night, my companion excused himself and entered the old farmhouse, leaving his rifle with me. For the first time I felt like a real soldier standing guard for my country. Shortly after I had taken up my new position, I noticed a dark shadow slipping from tree to tree about 150 feet away on the other side of the road.

Could this possibly be one of the German escapees we had been warned about? Raising my rifle, I aimed it at the shadow and called out in German, *"Wer ist da? Hände hoch!* (Who is there? Put your hands up)." There was no sound even after I fired a warning shot. Suddenly the shadow picked up speed and disappeared between the trees.

As soon as the actual fighting for control of the city had stopped and Allied forces captured the German garrison commander, the joy of the people knew no limits. Every block erupted into a spontaneous party with brightly glowing lights suspended from house to house. The happiness of the population suppressed for so long exploded into laughter, rejoicing, and singing. In thankfulness the citizens joined with hundreds of Canadian soldiers and danced tirelessly for days and nights to the music of phonograph records blasted out of hastily mounted loudspeakers. Husbands and loved ones long considered dead now emerged from their hiding places to tearfully embrace children and wives. "We thought you'd been killed, and now you're here. Thank God," was heard over and over again.

The war had ended. Our nightmare was finally over.

CHAPTER NINE

Aftermath

The euphoria we felt following the liberation was marred by the funeral of my friend, Henny. From my position in the procession, I could see the body rise and fall as we carried it to the grave site. The casket had no hinges, bolts, or metal handles. Only a piece of rope held it together, and I remember having doubts if it would even make it to the cemetery.

Many such funeral processions took place during those first few days after the war, for Groningen had lost a total of 106 of its citizens during the fighting.

But everyone was too happy to dwell long on the sadness. It did surprise all of us, however, when Uncle Max, after having survived the occupation, decided to forgive the enemy so completely that he and his wife Stiena adopted a little blond baby, the accidental result of the union of a Dutch girl and a German soldier. Ironically, this half-German child, now a six-foot-four man in his mid-40s with obvious Teutonic features and characteristics, bears the Jewish name Emil Israel. Both Max and his wife, as well as his entire family, are now dead. But his adopted son, my cousin, proudly carries on the name of Israel.

Ginus, my other uncle, the electronics engineer who spent all of the war years disguised as a woman, survived, only to die about five years later after falling from a telescoping ladder at a high-voltage construction job. Sadly enough, the role he had played while in hiding had become such an inseparable part of him that even after the war he could not rid himself of the habit of wearing women's undergarments and using makeup.

While we were living in Europe, my wife, Judie, and I tracked down the German army sergeant, Paul Dirksen, who had requisitioned our living room for a few months during the war. He had returned to his pre-war profession of motorcycle mechanic in the German seaport city of Emden and was still pro-German but definitely anti-Nazi. His wife, though American born, still praised Hitler's merits.

Flip, the Jewish fugitive whom we had sheltered for almost the entire duration of the occupation, worked in our upholstery shop for a while after the war until he found a better-paying job in Amsterdam. Shortly before his departure, he asked my mother for the use of our living room for a farewell party he wanted to give for the other upholsterers with whom he worked. The evening was a grand success. Everything had been catered, from pastries and hors d'oeuvre trays to a large whipped-cream cake. The pleasant memory of his farewell party lingered for many days—until the bills started coming in from the caterers addressed to my father. We had no choice but to pay them, but a few weeks after his departure from Groningen, my father happened to meet him on a sidewalk in Amsterdam. "Let's have lunch together, Mr. Noorbergen," Flip quickly suggested, and invited dad to one of the most luxurious restaurants in the city.

Halfway through their meal, Flip excused himself and asked a waiter for directions to the men's room. Determined not to be fooled again, dad grabbed Flip's jacket and pulled him back to his chair. "I learned my lesson in Groningen, Flip," he said. "You cannot pull this trick on me twice." When the waiter presented the check, Flip admitted that he was broke, and Dad and the management arrived at the perfect solution. They took him to the kitchen and ordered him to wash every dish in the restaurant for the next three days.

We never found out what happened to the SS deserter, Pieter de Vos, but Jack van der Mei, who stayed with us for a while during the war, became the housing administrator in Groningen. The shortage of affordable apartments has always been a problem for newlyweds in Holland, but after I married in 1961 and planned to make Groningen my base of operations for awhile, I was able to bypass the long waiting lists and lease a beautiful modern apartment overlooking the city only through the assistance of Jack van der Mei.

Once at 12:00 noon on May 5th while my wife, Judie, was admiring the view from our fifth floor apartment, she noticed a strange happening. Cars suddenly stopped wherever they were on the streets, bicyclists pulled to the side and dismounted, pedestrians halted on the sidewalk, and all bowed their heads in a moment of silent prayer in memory of those who died during the war. By designating May 5th as a national day of mourning, the people of Holland will never forget its heroes and the sacrifices they made to help our country regain its freedom.

My sister married her wartime sweetheart from Arnhem in 1948, and Fietje, who had broken her engagement with Pieter der Vos after the battle of Arnhem, married and moved to Haiti.

The fate of Arthur Seyss-Inquart, Hitler's representative for the Netherlands, was sealed during the International Military War Crimes Tribunal at Nürnberg in October 1946. It condemned him to death for his war crimes along with 23 other top Nazi war criminals. The death sentence took place on October 16. After the guards helped him to the platform, his final words were low and intense. "I hope that this execution is the last act of the tragedy of the Second World War, and that the lesson taken from this world war will be that peace and understanding should exist between peoples. I believe in Germany." Seyss-Inquart ascended the scaffold and dropped to his death at 2:45 a.m.

Fritz Sauckel, the slave labor boss who was responsible for forced labor in the occupied countries, preceded him in death. In Holland, Sauckel's brutal way of conscripting men to work in armament factories gave him the name of "little Hitler." It was to stay out of Sauckel's hands that my father had all of his teeth extracted in one sitting.

My father continued to lead an active life until he died at age 83. My mother, although she survived the war, was physically and mentally frail until her death in 1973. To her, the war did not end until shortly after the liberation when she heard the happy news, "The Valks are coming home." They were the Jewish family who had joined our church shortly before being shipped to a concentration camp. We

The author and his parents and sister immediately after the end of the war.

had never forgotten the sight of their entire family of two adults and six children, the youngest a small baby, tearfully saying goodbye at the railroad station as the guards loaded them on to the cattle cars.

Shortly after the liberation, we heard that returning Dutch Jews would arrive at the Harmonie, the city auditorium in the Boteringestraat, and my mother hurried ahead of all of us to catch the first glimpse of any member of the Valk family that might have survived. Dad and I followed on our bikes, arriving just as the first few long—distance buses had discharged their emaciated passengers. I immediately saw my mother pressing forward against the chain-link barriers the police had quickly erected.

"Jonas! We're here," she cried out loudly after seeing Mr. Valk and his wife Ria emerge from the processing line. "Oh, thank God, they survived, but what about the children?" Then she spotted their five teenage sons and daughters with one of the girls clutching the hand of her small 4-year-old sister. *They were all alive!* We couldn't believe it, yet there they all were together, the entire family, looking quite worn but alive. They had miraculously survived, and it was indeed a miracle as we soon learned.

After their arrival at their first concentration camp in Germany, the camp administration separated the family and sent its members to different camps. Throughout the four years, each member wondered whether he was the only one left of the family. As the Allies closed in, the Nazis decided to murder the last imprisoned Jews and assembled the remnants from other locations at one extermination camp. As they waited in line before entering the gas chamber, the entire Valk family was reunited, all eight of them. Tears flowed as they embraced for the last time, knowing that within minutes death would claim them all. Then the miracle happened. The gas supply ran out. American army units soon liberated the death camp.

Throughout her years of confinement, Ria Valk had somehow managed to conceal her baby in the barracks, and there the little one stood next to her brothers and sisters as living proof that miracles do happen. Today, even though Mr. and Mrs. Valk are no longer living, their children are all members of the Groningen Seventh-day Adventist Church.

My paternal grandmother, the aged courier, lived for many years after the war. I never had the opportunity, however, to meet my grandfather. I do remember my father coming home excited one afternoon several months after the liberation. He had just visited a resistance-fighters exhibit held in a large circus tent in one of the city squares. "You've got to come quickly," he exclaimed, running into the house. "Opa's picture is on one of the counterfeit *persoonsbewijzen* (identification cards) at the exhibit. He must have worked for the underground."

Queen Wilhelmina, whose faith in the ability of the Netherlands people sustained her during her wartime exile, died in 1962. At that time, her only child, Juliana, was already queen on the throne of the House of Orange, succeeding her mother after her 50-year reign. Juliana's eldest daughter, Beatrix, is the current queen.

In later years, Juliana's husband, Prince Bernhard, wartime leader of the Interior Forces, and I became and still are good friends.

Prince Bernhard with the author.

With the help of the Netherlands Union President, Hendrik Eelsing, the groundwork was laid for me to attend college in the U.S. after the war. Because of Dutch government regulations prohibiting anyone from taking guilders out of the country, Pastor Eelsing worked out an exchange of Dutch money at the church division office in Stockholm, Sweden, and returned with several hundred dollars worth of valuable Swedish kroner. With that and dollars my father had bought on the black market, I was able to pay my expenses for the first six months in the United States. Because the currency regulations also forbid taking foreign money out of Holland, I drilled deep holes underneath the hinges of my large steamer trunk into which I stuffed the rolled-up kroner and $100 bills.

Prior to my leaving, I had been taking a few correspondence courses from the Home Study Institute in Washington, D.C., whose administrator was Dr. M. E. Olson. The documents I needed for my entry into the United States was worked out with Dr. Shepherd, president of Washington Missionary College. During a conversation with my next-door neighbor, Louise Walther, at a potluck in Collegedale, Tennessee, 26 years later, I discovered to my surprise that

M. E. Olson was her father, and that she recalled his going to Union Station in the late '40s to meet a foreign student coming to the States for the first time.

Only after becoming a father did I understand the anguish my parents must have felt as they reluctantly allowed their only son to travel 6,000 miles to study history and journalism at La Sierra College in California. I can still remember seeing their worried looks as they watched me standing at the railing as the ship cast off for New York that misty June morning in 1947. For me, though, the great adventure was just beginning.

After finishing my schooling, I became a war correspondent for a number of international publications. Having lived amidst war during the formative years of my life, I felt strangely attracted to military confrontations such as those in Korea, the Middle East, Southeast Asia, Vietnam, Cuba, and other areas. As a foreign correspondent, I covered Fidel Castro's rise to power in Cuba, from his beginnings in the Sierra Maestra Mountains in the Oriente province of eastern Cuba to the presidential palace in Havana, then later followed the pro-Batista guerrillas in Miami planning his overthrow. It was there that I met and later married Judie, who was then secretary to the attorney representing the leading members of ousted President Batista's government.

Future assignments included covering the assassination of Generalissimo Hector Trujillo of the Dominican Republic, the Cuban missile crisis, the reign of terror by Haitian dictator "Papa Doc" Duvalier, the Suez Canal crisis, the U.S. interventions in Lebanon, the wars between Arabs and Israelis, the Berlin Blockade, the Hungarian Revolt, the escape of the Dalai Lama from Chinese-held Tibet, etc.

Much of the inner city of Groningen was destroyed in street fighting. Its aging heart was ripped out during the final battle of liberation. Centuries-old buildings with their Middle Ages facades fell prey to the hungry flames and the exchanges of gunfire between liberators and desperate occupiers. If it had not been defended so desperately, the inner city today would still have the appearance and feeling of old Amsterdam, which fortunately saw no fighting at all.

The canal in front of our house was filled in and has become a parking area. Today, still standing after 370 years, our wartime home is presently a women's health club. The interior has undergone considerable changes. However, its walls and basement still retain the secrets of their violent past.

Soon after the war we lost contact with Fietje, but an intermittent search for her, which I started in 1955, finally resulted in success in June 1990. Through a final plea for help issued by Clementine Puik of the program *Address Unknown* of KRO, the Dutch Catholic Broadcasting System, I discovered that she was currently living approximately 750 miles from my Tennessee home. Our reestablished contact refreshed many a dim memory of wartime events, such as the long-haired Canadian-Indian soldier who danced up and down like a harlequin in his successful attempt to escape the German machine gun bullets that were being sprayed at him.